The Secret Country
of C. S. Lewis

The Secret Country of C. S. Lewis

by

ANNE ARNOTT

Illustrations
by
Patricia Frost

Lakeland/Marshall Morgan & Scott
3, Beggarwood Lane, Basingstoke, Hants., UK.

Copyright © 1974 by Anne Arnot

First published by Hodder and Stoughton 1974.
This edition published by Marshall Morgan & Scott 1983.

ISBN 0 551 01062 2

Printed in Great Britain by
Cox & Wyman Ltd, Reading

Contents

'Most of us, I suppose, have a secret country . . .'

Voyage of the Dawn Treader, C. S. Lewis.

Prologue

ABOUT TWENTY YEARS AGO, A MAN SAT WRITING IN HIS BOOK-lined study at Magdalen College, Oxford, where he was a tutor and lecturer. His thoughts were turning back to far-off days, when he was a small boy. He had forgotten his many students to whom he had become almost a legend, had forgotten the troubles of his domestic life, and had laid aside his academic work. Scenes came before him with startling vividness, and as his pen moved swiftly over the page, his thoughts were fixed on his old home in Ireland, where he and his brother had invented a wonderful imaginary world for themselves.

Once more he seemed to be in the large house which was his home, while the rain poured relentlessly down outside, and splashed on the window-panes. The west wind sighed around the chimneys, and in imagination he picked up again an old stump of a candle, and climbed the stairs to the top of the house. Here he opened a door, and went inside an attic boxroom, remote and secret from the rest of the house. There he opened a certain little door where there was a cistern and a dark place behind it, into which he climbed. 'The dark place was like a long tunnel,' he wrote, 'with brick wall on one side and sloping roof on the other. In the roof there were little chinks of light between the slates. There was no floor in this tunnel: you had to step from rafter to rafter, and between them there was only plaster. If you stepped on this, you would find yourself falling through the ceiling of the room below.'

As he recalled those days, he was, in fact, writing a book for children called *The Magician's Nephew*, which you may know; and the secret hiding-place in the roof recalled from his boyhood days is woven into the story.

It is rather a special book because it describes the first adventures of the children who discovered the Kingdom of Narnia. There were to be seven books about this wonderful land, not only full of imaginary adventures and miraculous happenings, but more important still, the stories were full of many strange and true and beautiful hidden truths, all concerned with the great and eternal battle between good and evil. This has made the books unforgettable.

The man who was recalling the vivid days of his childhood spent with his brother, was to become known as a brilliant writer and story-teller, and an outstanding fighter for the Christian faith, in which he came to believe—only with difficulty—in his thirties. He had a wonderful gift for explaining it to ordinary people, some of whom did not read much, and for making it seem exciting and joyful, but never boring. Often he was asked to broadcast and to lecture about it, and wherever he went, or whatever he wrote, he made people think furiously. Sometimes he disturbed them; but he always stimulated them, so that often they were never quite the same again.

But now let us imagine we are standing unseen in his study, as he sits writing. The only sound is the comfortable crackling of the coal fire, and the slight scratch of the pen passing quickly across the sheets of paper. Outside the rooks call from the tree-tops near Magdalen Tower, and the bells of Oxford echo over the city. The great clocks chime the hours with deep full notes, and we are going backwards in time, to watch a boy grow up, and to enter his unknown world. We are going to watch him become a man with a mind like a sword that cut through all lies and sham, and showed up the blinding beauty of true goodness.

CHAPTER ONE

The Two Small Boys

IN IRELAND IT SEEMS TO RAIN INTERMINABLY. THAT IS WHY THE fields and mountains are so green, and some people call it 'The Emerald Isle'. At the end of the last century many parents were much more anxious about their children getting wet than they are today, and they wrapped them up or kept them indoors so that they should not catch colds or chills.

This memory of being imprisoned in a nursery, gazing out at the heavy slanting rain, and the sodden meadows, remained vividly in the minds of two small boys, Warren and Clive Lewis. Many years later they described it in their writings.

Clive was the younger. He was born in 1898, three and a half years after Warren, and two years before Queen Victoria died. As the boys grew out of babyhood, they were inseparable. Warren was often very protective towards Clive, who even at an early age was remarkably intelligent and had an unusually fertile and lively imagination. When they were kept in the house in bad weather, they used to write and draw constantly, and together they created an imaginary country, describing it in minute detail. As they gazed out of the window, they could see from their home the misty distant line of the Castlereagh hills, which they watched in changing weather, and which seemed to mark the end of their world, and often they wondered what lay beyond. It was then that they created their own land, plotting and planning its life and people. You could call it the land beyond the horizon, the land for ever out of sight. They called it Boxen. It was to become part of their life for many years.

Warren, the elder brother was of a rather more practical

turn of mind and drew mainly ships and trains, or described battles. I think he was always a soldier at heart. But Clive was the more fanciful. At first he drew 'dressed animals' as he called them, and his part of the creation was 'Animal Land'.

The boys' home was in a suburb of the great city of Belfast. Their father, Albert James Lewis, was a solicitor. He was a handsome man with a bushy moustache in the fashion of the day, and he was quite a formidable public speaker, gifted at oratory, and fascinated by politics. He was a great reader, and he loved to tell tales, and act the parts of the characters he described. Clive Lewis once said that his father was the best story-teller he had ever heard. But at heart he was rather an emotional and passionate man at the mercy of his moods, and sadly, he could not always understand his boys, although he was generous and kind to them.

Their mother, Flora Augusta Hamilton, was a clever woman, with great academic gifts. She came of a family that included clergymen, sailors and lawyers. She herself took a Bachelor of Arts degree at Queen's College, Belfast, when this was an uncommon achievement for women, compared with nowadays. She was really a mathematician, but she was also able to teach her small boys French and Latin as well. Like her husband, she, too, was a great reader, particularly of good novels. The house was unusually full of books, they overflowed onto landings and into the cloakroom, and were piled in many corners, but the boys were allowed to read any of them they wanted, and it was through books that they entered unknown worlds, and let their imaginations feast on what they discovered.

The boys' early years were very happy. Their parents were kind and loving. One early photograph shows their mother as having a merry intelligent sensible face. She is seen playing with the children and two small friends in the garden.

As was the custom of the day in professional men's families, the little boys had a nurse or nanny to look after them.

She was full of kindness and gaiety, and had a sort of earthy common-sense. A children's nurse, in those days, who worked in the wealthier families, could make or mar a child's life. But some loved their 'charges', as they called them with a devotion hardly rivalled by their mother, and Lizzie Endicott was one of these. She was an ordinary country girl from Co. Down, and she entered happily into the little boys' lives and gave them care and affection, and a knowledge of country things. There was a garden to play in, and they were never lonely because they always seemed to have so much to do together. When Clive was born, Warren once recalled that he had been rather jealous of the attention his mother had to give to the new arrival. But all this faded as they grew up together.

Their days were spent in a quiet routine, but there were certain highlights they never forgot. There was the intense excitement of the annual summer holiday at the seaside. No child to day, in an age of cars and planes and ceaseless swift travel from one end of the earth to the other can remotely picture the thrill of the yearly preparations for going away. It was a custom that had only become widespread in the nineteenth century with the coming of the railways, which opened up fascinating and hitherto unknown parts of the country to many people who had never travelled far from home. Generally a house would be rented for a month or so by a whole family at some seaside place. Sea air was thought to be very health-giving. Prior to the great day, vast domed trunks were filled with an extraordinary amount of luggage, and were often taken to the station on a carrier's horse-drawn cart, and the family, following in a cab or carriage, would climb into the train to set off for the great adventure of the year.

Warren and Clive were mainly with their mother on these happy holidays. Their father sometimes came down for a weekend, but never enjoyed it. He always had a rooted dislike of upsetting his daily routine in any way. If he came, he used to pace up and down the beach moodily, hands in pockets, yawning and looking at his watch, and he clearly found the life there tedious and a waste of time. Perhaps, at these times which were so happy for the boys, they became aware of their father's lack of understanding of them and of their pleasures. This was later to become a source of sadness and misunderstanding. But for the boys, the holidays remained in their minds as golden days, full of sunlight.

It was on holiday one year that Clive suddenly took a dislike to his name. He announced to his mother, pointing to himself, 'He is Jacksie'. From then on he stubbornly refused to answer to any other name. Eventually he became known as Jack to his family and all his friends for the rest of his life. So from now on, he will be known to us too, as Jack.

From a very early age Jack Lewis spent much of his time drawing, using his pencil and paints. Some of the pictures remain. They are full of movement, of people running or fighting. But, as he was to say in later years, neither he nor his brother at that time seemed to show any awareness or understanding of what was beautiful. And so he was to remember all his life a tiny event, apparently unimportant, when he first had a sudden stabbing realisation that something was beautiful. Yet it was such a little thing to make such a deep impression. Warren created a miniature forest or garden in the lid of a biscuit tin, which he had first covered with moss. In this he had planted twigs and flowers. Jack hung over this, gazing entranced. It was a tiny green secret world, sweetly scented of damp earth, and touched with sparkling drops of dew. In imagination he shrank into a tiny size, and pictured himself wandering in it. To him it seemed like Paradise. It gave him a special feeling. He was later to call this 'Joy'.

The boys grew up looking out at faraway hills, lonely and unspoilt under the wide empty sky. The dusty roads like white ribbons ran beneath them, and sometimes from far away they could hear the creak and rumble of the farm carts, often drawn by donkeys, as they rattled along in the distance.

Or they heard the stormy west winds shake the house, and sigh among the roof tops. Home seemed snug and cosy.

Both children were taught to say their prayers, and were taken regularly to church on Sundays, although Jack found the services rather boring. But the parents were not really strict for their day, and the children were only doing what was usual and customary at that time. They accepted it all as a normal part of a happy settled secure life.

Jack's only remembered unhappiness in those very early days was his terrifying dreams, and this is, perhaps, proof of his too vivid imagination. Sometimes he dreamed about ghosts, and sometimes about insects. The latter were the most horrifying. Even when he was grown-up, he recalled those dreams, and said, 'To this day I would rather meet a ghost than a tarantula (spider).'

So perhaps it is not surprising that when in middle-age he wrote one of his wonderful science fiction novels, which, like his books for children, were to have great and beautiful truths underlying the story, he recalled a horrible moment, and described it happening to the hero of the story: 'Once, as he had sat writing near an open window in Cambridge, he had looked up and shuddered to see, as he supposed, a many coloured beetle of unusually hideous shape crawling across his paper . . .' In this book, *Voyage to Venus*, the interesting thing is that, almost as if in a battle, the hero learns to conquer this unreasoning fear for ever. In a way, much of Jack Lewis's life was to be a battle of the spirit.

But those first early years were to be peaceful and secure. There was always someone ready to comfort Jack in his fears, and he was safe and happy in his home.

CHAPTER TWO

The New House

WHEN JACK WAS SEVEN YEARS OLD HIS PARENTS MOVED TO 'Little Lea', a new house on the edge of Belfast. On one side the house lay beside open farmland. At the front they looked down over open fields to Belfast Lough, and away beyond the glinting stretch of water there rose the mountains of Antrim. Behind the house were the Holywood hills. Away to the west the boys often gazed across the vast blue ridges, lying in fold after fold. Here, they watched the long brilliant sunsets, touching the hills with gold and shimmering the fields with unearthly splendour. They could see the rooks flying home in the evening, black specks against the gold and red sky, calling harshly to each other; and haunting and melancholy, there often came up from the waters of the lough, the hooting from the ships as they passed to and fro, and it brought thoughts of romantic journeys and far countries.

The house itself had a character of its own. Mr. Lewis, who had evidently been prospering in his legal practice, had decided to build this much larger house, so that the family might live farther out towards the country. The builders did not, in fact, make a particularly good job of it for, as Jack later recorded, 'My father—had more capacity for being cheated than any man I have ever known.' So the drains were poor and the chimneys unsatisfactory, and the house was full of draughts, but to the children it was wonderful. It was a house of real character, and all through his life Jack was to return to it nostalgically in memory, remembering its oddities, its spaciousness, and the sun pouring in, or the rain from the west beating wildly against the window panes. Many years later he wrote about it: 'I am a product of long

corridors, empty sunlit rooms, upstair indoor silences, attics
explored in solitude, distant noises of gurgling cisterns and
pipes, and the noise of wind under the tiles.'

In this house the boys' writing flourished. Boxen and
Animal-Land grew more and more important. It was an
excitement and joy for the boys to have their very own
special room in the attic, instead of having one room only as
nursery and bedroom combined. For in those days many
children did not have the run of the house as they do now.
They were still expected to be 'seen and not heard', or else
not seen at all, unless their parents sent for them to join them
in the drawing-room or dining-room. Nannies or maids
had to watch over them. So the new attic spelled freedom,
because no maids interfered with their doings up there, or
kept tidying up their things. Away in their secret retreat they
were lost to sight and sound. It was quite a fascinating
kingdom of their own up in the roof. There were the little
passages through which they could crawl, and secret cavernous hiding-places like the little cistern-room which, as you
know, became the model for the beginning of the adventures
in *The Magician's Nephew*.

Nevertheless, life began to change for the boys after they
came to the new house. First, Warren was sent away to
boarding school in England. At first Jack did not mind so
much, because his own life went on happily. He had his
lessons from his mother still, and from a rather gentle and
and meek little governess, Annie Harper. She does not seem
to have made much impression on him, although she taught
him well and thoroughly all the subjects which he did not
do with his mother.

He did not feel really lonely because the house was full
of people. There were his parents, and his grandfather on
father's side, an old deaf man, who walked slowly around the
house, often humming Psalm tunes. He was rather fussy,
and often used to get agitated about his health, and had a
habit of trying to get sympathy by telling one member of the
family after another that he had not much longer time with

them. There were the maids too, bustling around the house, and the gardener who was thought to be too fond of drink. Other relatives lived near enough to visit, and became vivid characters in Jack's life.

There was Uncle Gussie, his mother's kindly brother, who used to talk to the boys as equals, as if they understood grown-up matters. He had a Canadian wife, Aunt Annie, always cheerful and welcoming. There was Uncle Joe, Mr. Lewis's elder brother, with his two boys and three girls living near to their old house. He was a kind and clever man. But on the whole the grown-ups seemed a little remote to Jack as they always seemed to be talking about dull things like politics or health, or business affairs.

More important to Jack than his close relatives was the exciting family who lived less than a mile away at the biggest house he knew, which he calls Mountbracken. Lady E. was his mother's first cousin. Her husband, Sir W. E., known as Cousin Quartus, was a gracious kindly man who had a beard and a handsome noble face. Lady E. or Cousin Mary, was beautiful herself with silver hair and a soft melodious Southern Irish voice. But the three daughters were like goddesses to Jack, so striking were they: and one of them, the youngest, Jack later called 'the most beautiful woman I have ever seen'. The boys often visited Mountbracken. Jack was taken for walks there. The great thrill was going for drives in the 'motor-car', a comparatively new invention then, and there were picnics and theatre visits. Because they were treated so kindly and graciously at Mountbracken, the small boys were always on their best behaviour there. Anything else would have been unthinkable.

Among all these grown-up people Jack moved happily, chattering away to everyone around him. But at heart, after Warren went to school, he was conscious of his solitariness. I do not think it bothered him at first. For like many lonely children, he created his own secret life and imaginary world, and for him it centred around the stories he wrote so constantly, and all the books he read.

But one thing worried and frustrated him very much. He was very clumsy with his hands. He had a defect inherited from his father: he had only one joint in the thumb. He constantly longed to make things with scissors out of cardboard, glue and paper, things like ships or houses or engines. But however often he tried, it was no good. He began to feel a failure, and sometimes wept tears of angry desperation. And so he was driven to do the one thing he excelled at: to write down the stories and adventures which packed his inventive brain. He never dreamed that his foot was on the first step of a ladder leading to fame, and that through this he would become known in many parts of the world.

Writing is, in a way, a secret pleasure. It can relieve the feelings, and release pent-up tensions and emotions. Given the will, there is almost no one of ordinary intelligence who cannot find relief in it. Children who are encouraged to write for sheer pleasure often find a rare happiness. But it is best to have a quiet place where you can be alone. Jack found the attic perfect. Eventually it became his 'study', and the very word made him feel grown-up. He nailed coloured pictures from the Christmas numbers of magazines to the walls. He stored away up there his pens, notebooks and paint-box. Here he wrote and illustrated his stories. At first they were mainly about what he called 'dressed animals', and 'knights-in-armour'. But the high-spots in Jack's life came when Warren arrived home for the holidays. Then his writing had to fit into his brother's ideas and interests, and Warren's thoughts centred on trains and steam ships. So Jack had to adapt Animal-Land to take in these modern inventions. He quickly evolved a plan, Animal-Land would have to be brought up to date. He would write its history. At this time Warren's country, which figured in all his stories, was India. India and Animal-Land had, therefore, to be connected, and together formed Boxen. Maps had to be drawn, steamships routes were charted by Warren, the landscape was described and filled with many imaginary characters, some being almost unconscious caricatures of friends and relatives.

It is interesting to note that another family of brilliant children, often shut indoors, had done the same thing many years before. The Brontës, shut up in Haworth parsonage in the wild Yorkshire winters, also invented their own imaginary country. Perhaps many of you have, too.

When Jack and Warren were not inventing and writing down their own stories, there was the inexhaustible supply of books to draw on. Years later Jack described them piled around the house; there were 'books in the study, books in the drawing-room, books in the cloakroom, books (two deep) in the great bookcase on the landing, books in a bedroom, books piled as high as my shoulder in the cistern attic, books of all kinds reflecting every transient stage of my parents' interests, books readable and unreadable, books suitable for a child, and books most emphatically not'. But none were barred to the boys, and they feasted on everything to their taste, and let their imaginations wander in new worlds.

Some of these books you may have read yourselves. They liked books by Conan Doyle who invented Sherlock Holmes. There were E. Nesbit's famous children's books; *The Railway Children*, is still well-known, but Jack's favourite was *The Amulet*, because it made him aware of distant ages, and the mystery of the past. He loved *Five Children and It* and *The Phoenix and the Wishing Carpet*, because tales of mystery and magic appealed to him so much. He also enjoyed *Gulliver's Travels* by Swift. A wonderful set of old *Punch* magazines kept him occupied for hours. Strangely, too, he turned back again and again to favourites from very early days, the Beatrix Potter books. Many children remember Squirrel Nutkin, Jemima Puddleduck, Tom Kitten and the rest, and may have examined those delicate and beautiful little pictures just faintly suggesting in their backgrounds the landscape and countryside of Cumberland where Beatrix Potter lived.

It was while examining the pictures of Squirrel Nutkin, that Jack—small as he was—suddenly became aware of beauty again. It was as if he was now looking out for it, almost unconsciously, and there in the tiny pictures representing the autumn woods, he found it. He gazed and gazed entranced. The feeling of enchantment came back just as it had when he saw the tiny garden in the biscuit-tin lid.

Soon after this, he had an experience which showed him that actually reading certain words could bring back this awareness of beauty. He picked up an unknown book. We can imagine him, in the silent attic, poring over words he could not even understand. They were quite unrelated to any experience he had ever had, or any scene he knew, but somehow they transported him in imagination, and he found himself seeing in his mind's eye an immense pale remote northern sky. The words echoed in his mind, filling it with a sort of pain and longing for he knew not what. The words were:

> I heard a voice that cried,
> Balder the beautiful
> Is dead, is dead

—and they echoed hauntingly in his mind. Balder, in Scandinavian mythology was a son of Odin, the supreme god and creator. He was beloved by all, and died through the treachery of Loki. Jack knew none of this, nor who Balder was. But, sensitive to the power of the words, they drew out in him that awareness again which years later he came to call 'Joy'. It was hard to define this, but he felt a longing for something which could not be reached.

So Jack's days passed; and often he retreated into this secret world up in the attics. It was because he remembered those days so vividly that later he could re-create them for us in his books. The details of that cistern attic, which were related in *The Magician's Nephew*, were described as if it belonged to a girl called Polly. This is what we read:

> Polly had used the bit of the tunnel just beside the cistern as a smuggler's cave. She had brought up bits of old packing cases and the seats of broken kitchen chairs, and things

of that sort, and spread them across from rafter to rafter so as to make a bit of floor. Here she kept a cash-box containing various treasures, and a story she was writing, and usually a few apples. She had often drunk a quiet bottle of ginger-beer in there: the old bottles made it look more like a Smuggler's Cave.

It was a quiet happy life for Jack. It seemed as if it was likely to go on in this peaceful pattern for a long time. But in 1908, the happy times suddenly ended. The boys' world was to change drastically and sadly. Nothing was ever to be quite the same again.

CHAPTER THREE

The Great Loss

JACK WAS TEN YEARS OLD WHEN THE HAPPY DAYS IN THE New House came to an end. The whole house seemed at the time almost to change its character. The nights were full of fears. Whispered anxious voices could often be heard, strange sounds of coming and going in his mother's room where she lay pale and ill. Although she was still comparatively young, she had developed cancer. It was a terrible time. She was operated on, not in a hospital but in her home as often happened in those days, and the doctor's and surgeon's frequent visits, the strange smells of anaesthetic, and disinfectant, and the anxiety of every member of the household, terrified the small boy.

After the operation she seemed better for a time. Jack used to go softly into her room, gazing at her as she lay in bed, and his heart was full of anxious hope that she must surely be getting better. He noticed how pale and thin she looked, and he would take her things which he thought would make her better. Then she relapsed, and passed into a state of fever and delirium; or else she would be drowsy under the influence of pain-killing morphia.

Jack spent much time putting up fervent desperate prayers for her recovery. He was sure God would perform a miracle. Now the boys were shut away from her, and life was sinister and fearful, with listening and watching and wondering. Soon the boys were told the terrible news that she would not recover. But Jack set himself to believe that the miracle he prayed for so earnestly would undoubtedly occur.

One night he was tired and sick himself, and he tossed and turned in bed with headache and toothache. He longed for his mother; he called for her, but she did not come, as she always had when he needed her. Then he became aware of doors opening and shutting, whispered voices again, people walking to and fro, and dread crept over him. He began to cry bitterly for his mother, but no one came.

At last, late in the night, as if in a nightmare, he saw his father come into the room in tears. This horrified him. It was as if the foundations of his life were crumbling away. Presently his father told him the unbelievable and terrible news. His mother was dead. It seemed to Jack as if a whole continent that one had thought utterly firm, had suddenly sunk beneath the waves and one was left floundering like a drowning man in the deep waters of a wide sea, studded only with distant islands, for which one had to strike out over the perilous waves, if one was ever to survive.

Jack now felt that his prayers for his mother's recovery must be changed immediately. He would pray for another miracle, that she should be restored to life. For a time he really believed this would happen. When it did not, his childish faith withered within him. The whole thing did not work. Years later he was to write that in those terrible days, he had approached God as if he was some great magician, but that he had never, for one moment, had any idea of the tremendous power he was trying to harness to his own small hopes and earnest desires. He really knew nothing of God, and had no idea what it meant to love Him. All he knew was, that in one night, the light in his life was extinguished. He was groping in the dark.

The horror of the whole situation was deepened, when, as was then the custom, Jack was taken into the room where his mother lay dead, to say farewell to her. It was a terrifying moment, and the fear of it went far deeper than anyone knew. He was never to forget it. He became distracted by the dreadful paraphernalia of the funeral: the hearse, the coffin, the flowers. He fought frenziedly not to wear the heavy dark clothes of mourning that were then customary, and he became greatly distressed. In a short time, as he

recorded later, 'all settled happiness was gone'. His father could not comfort him. He, too, was distracted with grief, and his temper became uncertain. He was never fully to recover from the loss of his wife. Sometimes he began to seem very unjust. The two small frightened boys drew closer and closer together, and withdrew for comfort into a world of their own imagining.

When in middle life, Jack was sitting in that quiet study at Oxford, writing *The Magician's Nephew*, he was able to go right back again in memory to those dreadful days, and to re-live them in the person of Digory. At the beginning of the book Digory is found tear-stained and unhappy, in the care of an aunt and a strange eccentric uncle, who were looking after his dying mother, while his father was away in India. His passionate desire to find a cure for her, runs through the whole book. It leads him into great and perilous adventures, in which he overcomes his fears and failings, and seeks and finds the Apple of Life, which he obtains at peril of his own life.

How tenderly the moment is described when he takes it into his mother's room. We can trace the echo of Jack's desperate longing as a small boy to save his own mother: 'Then Digory took a moment to get his breath and then went softly into his mother's room. And there she lay, as he had seen her lie so many times, propped up on the pillows, with a thin pale face that would make you cry to look at it.'

He took the apple out of his pocket, and noticed that everything seemed colourless beside it, and it threw strange and beautiful lights on the ceiling as he turned it in his hand. It had a sweet and fragrant smell so that it seemed as if 'there was a window in the room that opened on Heaven'.

'Oh, darling, how lovely,' said Digory's mother. He persuades her to try and eat it, and cuts it up for her, and she falls into a much-needed refreshing sleep. If you read the book to see what happened, you will feel Digory's passionate anxiety to help his mother, and you will know that this writing comes deep from the heart of its author, drawn out of his own past sorrow.

CHAPTER FOUR

The Prison House

THE LIGHTS WERE STARTING TO SHINE OUT FROM THE SHOPS and terrace houses of Belfast one evening in September, 1908. The pavements were damp from recent rain. Horse-drawn cabs and carriages clattered past each other over the cobbled city roads. Workmen were making for home, and people were settling down to their evening leisure. One four-wheeler cab rattled along at a steady pace and turned into the drearier part of the town and headed towards the docks. Inside sat a solemn rather distinguished-looking man with a gloomy preoccupied expression, and beside him were two small boys.

Mr. Lewis was taking his sons to see them off on the night ferry for England where Jack was going to join Warren at boarding school. Warren was by now a veteran traveller on this journey, but for Jack who had only recently lost his mother, and was not quite eleven years old, it was a rather grim new experience. For one thing, he felt extraordinarily uncomfortable in his new school clothes. He had played happily enough in the morning, pushing away to the back of his mind the thought of leaving home, and had worn his old comfy clothes, blazer, shorts and socks. Now he was forced to wear a thick prickly suit of some heavy serge type of material, and he had knickerbockers on, which buttoned so tightly just below the knee, that the button left a red mark in his flesh. He had on a stiff white Eton collar, as was the custom for public schoolboys, and he had heavy stiff new boots which made his feet ache. Worst of all, pressed hard on his head so that he felt as if he was gripped by an iron band, was a horrid hard bowler hat. He felt as if he was a prisoner in this uniform.

At last the swaying cab turned onto the quay where the old Fleetwood boat lay tossing gently on the lightly moving water. The dark cavernous interior of the cab, smelling of leather and horse, seemed a secret shelter. It was another step into the unknown when Jack stepped down onto the iron step, and then to the ground. Father and sons went up the gang plank and aboard. For the first time, as he felt the breeze off the lough touch his face, Jack felt a little excited. The journey itself was a new adventure for him. But Mr. Lewis who paced up and down the deck beside the boys, was obviously so deeply moved and upset at losing them both, that it depressed the boys greatly. Jack's father was, indeed, much to be pitied. Not only had he lost his young wife, but also his old father and a brother had died within the year. Now he felt it was his duty to send his two small boys away to be well educated. There is no doubt he was a very lonely man. But the boys were embarrassed to see the signs of his grief. They had clung together since their mother died, and were learning to hide their own sense of forlornness. It was only an opening of the wound to see their father so distressed. Jack had become frightened by any show of emotion since his mother's death. So at last when he finally turned and left them, they were relieved.

Jack began to cheer up and take an interest in the novelty of his first sea-crossing, and he wanted to explore the boat with Warren. He felt the first tinge of pleasure. This was a real adventure. Warren had not the heart to disillusion him, for he knew what sort of life was waiting for them. So he went about the boat with Jack, who peered through the skylight above the engine-room, and smelt the hot oily smell from below. He hung with him over the side as the ship's melancholy hooting proclaimed she was about to cast off. Then the boys heard the first throbbing of the screws, and the chugging of the engines. At last, slowly, imperceptibly, the land seemed to draw away. The lights from the harbour grew smaller, and there came that slight rolling movement underfoot that experienced travellers recognise, which never

ceases to be a thrill as the boat moves out, and the air freshens. As the boat headed down the lough, the harbour lights became distant pinpoints in the darkness.

Suddenly Jack tasted salt on his lips. It was a moment he was never to forget, and he was to watch for it on other journeys. The movement of the ship grew more pronounced. They were at sea, and had left the harbour mouth. The ship began to toss in a stiffening wind. Jack felt his old life was slipping away, and with it everything that was known and safe.

The boys went down to their bunks, and the swell of the sea grew stronger. Warren became sea-sick. Jack felt this was a very grown-up performance by an experienced traveller, and tried to be sick too. But it was only as the night wore on that he became slightly sick himself. All through his life he was to remain what he called an obstinately good sailor.

Early the next morning, the grey flat shores of England came into view, and at about six o'clock they left the boat. As they travelled south by train, Jack who had grown up near hills and mountains was appalled by the dullness of the English landscape. He missed the cosy little white farmhouses, the stone walls and tiny fields. It was all wrong. The landscape seemed monotonously flat. He was cut off from the sea as the train rushed onwards, and he felt an alien in a hateful land. It was a feeling that was to last quite a long time.

The school to which the boys were travelling was a small preparatory school. It was run by an extraordinary man whom the boys called Oldie. Years later Jack wrote this vivid description of him. He said he was a 'big bearded man with full lips like an Assyrian King on a monument, immensely strong, physically dirty'. In fact the man was cruel, and only seven years before had had a High Court action brought against him for his brutal treatment of a boy. This was eventually settled privately out of court, but by 1908 the school had dwindled in numbers to some sixteen to eighteen boys, half of them boarders, the rest day-boys. The school was, in fact, well on the way to final collapse.

Mr. Lewis, with what Warren, looking back in later years described as his 'uncanny flair for making the wrong decision' had, by some error of judgment, picked as bad a school as well he could, to which to send his motherless boys.

Jack found himself in a nightmare world when he arrived at the school which later he nicknamed Belsen, after the German Concentration Camp, where terrible atrocities took place during the Second World War. Belsen was a school where all organised games had been given up, although this particular thing did not worry him so much as the large classroom where the well-used canes hung on the green iron mantelpiece. These were to remind the boys daily of their fate if they failed to answer Oldie's questions.

'Bring me my cane, I see I shall need it,' Oldie would shout, when some unfortunate boy angered him.

The teaching was shared between Oldie's son, nicknamed Wee-wee, and a succession of unfortunate young assistants or ushers as they were then called, all of whom left after a short time, one actually within a week. Once one so enraged Oldie that he said to him that if he had not been in Holy Orders—a clergyman—he would have kicked him downstairs.

At mealtimes Oldie and Wee-wee sat at a special table, and ate special food and drank beer. Oldie's silent wife and three silent daughters all dressed in black, sat with them, eating inferior food. The daughters were never heard to say more than 'Yes, Papa', or 'No, Papa.'

The lessons were quite inadequate, and badly taught, except for geometry which Oldie taught well, but with cruelty to his pupils.

Jack found he was not as badly off as those boys who were Oldie's chief victims, whom he flogged unmercifully. On the whole they were the boys who came from below a certain social class. Jack watched horrified and fascinated, his mind like a slate on which vivid and terrible pictures were drawn.

In later years when he recalled them, he seemed to re-live them again, and he entered once more in retrospect the gloomy classroom; and he saw 'Poor P.—dear, honest hardworking friendly, healthily pious P.—endure thrashing after thrashing for no good reason, and he recorded the agonising moment when 'towards the end of the torture, there came a noise quite unlike a human utterance. That peculiar croaking or rattling cry, that, and the grey faces of all the other boys, and their deathlike stillness, are among the memories I could willingly dispense with.'

It was an unbelievable situation. Mr. Lewis clearly had no idea how bad a school it was. Indeed, in the past boys had won many scholarships to public schools. But it seemed probable that Oldie was now on the verge of insanity.

During the nights in this prison, Jack's thoughts—restricted during the day to lessons and to the mass of dull information about dates, battles and exports with which the boys' minds were crammed—roamed far and wide. In the great curtainless dormitory he used to gaze out at the night sky, and he felt like a prisoner behind bars. As the days and months went by, he experienced violent extremes of weather, unknown to him in the milder Irish climate. He watched tremendous thunderstorms, saw fog swirling and eddying round the school, felt the freezing cold of a bitter winter with frost and snow. Ever and again he gazed out of the tall windows spellbound by 'the ghastly beauty of the full moon', as he described it. The vast canopy of the dark night sky was full of mystery and magic to him. The cold remote light of the moon touched the black skeletons of trees and the jumbled shapes of houses, seeming to turn them into another enchanted world and his imagination was fired by this thought.

Sitting in his quiet study at Oxford many years later, where we first watched him, he used to recall those days. The fascination of the night sky and the moonlight casting eerie shadows and bewitching everything around, is often reproduced in his stories. Many of the adventures he wrote about took place by moonlight. Sometimes the moon is full, sometimes partly hidden behind clouds. The different children about whom he writes all echo his boyhood feelings. All dislike school, and find marvellous adventures often at night time. Jill Pole, in the book called *The Silver Chair*, is just beginning a term in a horrid school. Suddenly she is carried away by magic to the heart of Narnia and is commissioned with Eustace Scrubb by the great lion Aslan, to find the lost Prince Rilian. She has to fly through the night on the back of a great owl, and somehow, because the story is so skilfully written, it does not seem impossible at all. This is what happens:

As soon as the lamp was out, the bit of the night which you saw through the window looked less dark no longer black, but grey. The owl stood on the window-sill, with his back to the room and raised his wings. Jill had to climb on his short fat body and get her knees under the wings and grip tight. The feathers felt beautifully warm and soft but there was nothing to hold on by . . .

It was much lighter than she had expected, and though the sky was overcast, one patch of watery silver showed where the moon was hiding above the clouds. The fields beneath her looked grey, and the trees black. There was a certain amount of wind—a hustling, ruffling sort of wind which meant that rain was coming soon.

When you read the Narnia stories for yourself, think of the small boy, Jack Lewis, gazing out at the night sky at school, studying it, and watching the sombre colours of darkness in all their variations so closely, that years later he could clearly reproduce them again in his mind and see them just as they were when he was small; so that he was able to bring them to life again in his writing. He can create, too, an immense scenic background of natural beauty, of which all his life he was so vividly aware, against which the events of his stories can be fittingly played out.

The terms dragged cruelly and interminably at Oldie's. The last day seemed as if it would never come. But when at last it dawned, then Jack knew bliss. He could forget the beatings which he saw his friends endure—he himself seems to have got off comparatively lightly; he could forget all the discomfort, the terrible feeling of imprisonment, and the general misery, and give himself up to the excitement of setting out once more on the long journey by train and boat to his home and freedom.

Yet he grew up to believe there were some things of value that he learned at Belsen. Just as he had drawn so close to his brother in their utter misery at their mother's death, so now he drew close to the few other boys with whom he was left in the school when his brother went on to a big public school. Together on half-holidays, the boys at Oldie's wandered by the canal, bought sweets in the quiet village shops, and sat on the grassy bank above a railway cutting watching the dark gaping tunnel mouth for trains. He was learning to be one of a group of friends, all up against it, and therefore all the closer to each other.

Perhaps even more important, although it did not appear significant then or for years later, Jack started to believe in Christianity. In his misery, he got some comfort from the parish church where the boys were taken. Sunday by Sunday he listened intently, and was to record that there he first heard Christian teaching put forward in a compelling way, by men who were totally committed to their faith. Now the sight of the night sky gripped him more, and for a new reason. He began to believe in Hell, and at nights 'especially on certain blazing moonlight nights in that curtainless dormitory' he began to have childish fears for his soul.

Quite naturally he began to read his Bible, and to pray fervently. He began to discuss religion with some of the other boys in quite a straightforward way, for he was always questioning, probing deeper into problems than most boys. He was never going to be satisfied until he found the right answers.

He did not know then, how hard the journey into understanding would ultimately be.

CHAPTER FIVE

Interlude

THE TIME CAME WHEN MR. LEWIS HAD TO FIND ANOTHER school for Jack. Oldie's school eventually closed down which was not surprising. Jack had clearly been so unhappy that Mr. Lewis decided to keep him near home, and he eventually decided to send him to Campbell College, Belfast. Mr. Lewis had thumbed through prospectuses of many schools before he came to this decision and consulted various professional friends. He was earnestly anxious to do his best for the boys, and it was clear his first choice had been disastrous. Jack was not, in any case, an entirely easy boy to place. Brilliant, highly-strung, imaginative, difficult to handle, and needing a mother badly, he may well have given his father much anxiety. It was Mr. Lewis's great desire, and this was typical of most professional men of the time, that his sons should learn to grow up as 'gentlemen', that they should both learn courtesy and culture, and be able to take their place in the world with dignity and ease. It was, however, impractical to hope that any school alone could achieve this. Campbell College also was to prove a disappointment to him.

But Jack was overjoyed. He was to join one of his cousins there, a son of Uncle Joe, and although he was to be a boarder, he was to come home every Sunday. No school in Ireland he thought, could ever be as unhappy as one in England.

Jack was twelve when he went to Campbell College. Perhaps school life there was not quite what he expected. The size of the school, the lack of studies, the constant movement and noise each day of crowds of boys, trooping to and fro from the enormous 'Prep' room, where they worked in the evenings, around the bare brick passages, and herding together in store rooms, in lavatories, and in the hall, made him feel as if he was living in a huge railway station. It was a school where there were many fights conducted with seconds, and betting, and yelling shouting crowds of spectators.

There was bullying, but Jack was not much affected by it except on one surprising occasion. Gangs of boys often roamed through the passages, searching for prey. One day Jack found himself with a number of other younger boys being dragged and pushed along a passage, and then shut into a low dark room. Pipes ran along one wall, about three feet from the floor. Jack saw in the half darkness that one boy was made to place his head beneath the pipes, and two of the gang then gave him a great shove, whereupon he instantly vanished. Jack was completely surprised. Where had he gone? The same thing happened to another boy, and then Jack was made to put his head beneath the pipes. He was given a hard shove and felt himself falling . . . He landed in the coal cellar beneath, through a hole he had not seen in the half darkness. There was eventually quite a little crowd of captured boys, and they found they were locked in. Huddled together in the chilly darkness they had to wait until, after what seemed an age, their captors consented to let them out, dirty but none the worse.

So boys at Campbell had to learn to fight for themselves, and to stand up for themselves, but some of the teaching was excellent. Jack was taught English Literature by an outstanding master he called Octie, through whom he first became fascinated by English poetry. He found that language could move him deeply. Certain words could fill his imagination with huge pictures, and he was greatly stirred by the narrative poem 'Sohrab and Rustum', written by Matthew Arnold, which tells the tale of the great Persian national hero, Rustum, a conqueror in war and combat, who unknowingly kills his own son. The poem begins with fog swirling up from the River Oxus, and the scene gives a feeling of remoteness. When he read this poem Jack was spellbound by this feeling of distance and by the strangeness of the Persian scenes, and the pedlars from Khabul, as well as by the description of the desert wastes. He felt as if through someone else's eyes he was gazing with emotion at things that were in a far country. It brought back this feeling of longing, a longing for something unattainable yet ever to be pursued. It was this awareness of an inexplicable desire, the very thought of which brought gladness to the mind, that he came to call 'Joy'. He reacted to this beauty in words just as he had to the miniature garden in the lid of a biscuit tin, and to the little pictures of autumn scenes in Squirrel Nutkin. Once he felt the same sense of delight when he saw a flowering currant bush in full bloom.

Some people experience a sudden *awareness* of beauty. It may come unexpectedly, at a time when one never expected such a thing, and one says, '*that* experience, *that* scene, was suddenly significant to me. It was a golden moment. When it passed, it was like a glory that has faded.' But however it comes, one is always eager to discover it again.

Jack was so alive to all he read in books, and so full of his own ideas and imaginings that he was impatient of people who could not understand or share his feelings. At this time he and his brother had no friends of their own age at home, and even avoided other people, especially one boy called Arthur who tried to get to know them. At home his life was so full, especially in the holidays when Warren was with him, walking and cycling in the countryside in fine weather, or reading and writing, that both boys resented the well-meant hospitality of neighbours and friends who invited them to parties and dances. It was torment to Jack to be dressed in his best clothes, to have to talk about utterly trivial uninteresting things to people with whom he had nothing in common. He began to feel he must be an odd man out, because all he longed for was to get into the horse-drawn cab which would take them home, bored and tired from some evening party. He felt it was all a horrible waste of time. Perhaps the fact that he felt he was clumsy added to this, for it was another thing that made him very sensitive.

When he met other people at social functions, Jack found that people laughed at his rather bookish language and grown-up talk, which of course came quite naturally to him. Always sensitive, he learned to adopt a mask. He made his own rule never to speak about anything in which he was really interested. Instead he put on what he called 'a giggling and gurgling imitation of the vapidest grown-up chatter, a deliberate concealment of all that I really thought . . .'

Jack learned to take life at Campbell College quite philosophically, and actually enjoyed the work. By now he was toughening up, and learned that at this school like many others, 'every boy held just the place which his fists and mother-wit could win for him', as he wrote later. But halfway through the term he fell ill, and eventually was sent home to recover. It was now that he experienced one of the only satisfying and happy periods of life with his father. The two, alone together, drew very close. Mr. Lewis was evidently sympathetic about Jack's acute night fears, which almost certainly stemmed from his deep distress at his mother's death and his fear of his father's anger when he used to pour forth a flood of oratory and gloom. Basically too kind to strike the boys, he used this other weapon almost unconsciously, as Jack later said; and when he was angered 'all the resources of his immense vocabulary were poured forth'. He used to imply that if the boys' behaviour did not improve, and they did not do better, they would all be ruined, and they would be begging for bread in the streets. It was all a way of relieving his temper, but Jack believed it, and he became deeply anxious and nervous. Some nights he awoke and could not hear Warren's breathing, and he would be gripped by dreadful fears. Warren must have got up and gone away to America with his father, they must have left Jack behind. His highly-coloured imagination used to run riot, but under

—lying it all was fear—fear of being 'left' again, as his mother had left him when he so greatly needed her.

So when he came home ill from school, Mr. Lewis for once showed a rare understanding. He had Jack's bed put in his own room, and without Warren to come between them, there was no friction. Jack was full of affection for his father. 'I remember no other time in my life of such untroubled affection,' he said. 'We were famously snug together.'

When his father was out by day, leaving only the maids in the house, Jack revelled in the silence and emptiness of the house after the crowds and ceaseless noise of Campbell College. He began to read fairy tales again, although twelve years old, stories which had fascinated him when he was younger. He fell under the spell of 'the little people' and in particular the Dwarfs. He visualised them with such intensity that when he was better and walking in the garden one day, he suddenly thought he saw one run past him into the shrubbery, but he was not afraid.

Years later he wrote about this taste for 'the land of faerie':

When I was ten, I read fairy tales in secret and would have been ashamed if I had been found doing so. Now that I am fifty I read them openly. When I became a man I put away childish things, including the fear of childishness and the desire to be very grown up.

And so the year 1910 ended fairly happily for Jack. January, 1911, was to see yet another change for him.

CHAPTER SIX

The Dark Ages

ONCE THERE WERE FOUR CHILDREN WHOSE NAMES WERE Peter, Susan, Edmund, and Lucy . . . and now all four of them were sitting on a seat at a railway station with trunks and playboxes piled up round them. They were, in fact, on their way back to school . . . The first part of the journey, when they were all together, always seemed to be part of the holidays; but now when they would be saying good-bye and going different ways so soon, everyone felt that the holidays were really over, and everyone felt their term-time feelings beginning again, and they were all rather gloomy . . .

When you read these words in that wonderful tale of adventure and mystery, *Prince Caspian*, by C. S. Lewis, you can tell that it is, in a sense, the young Jack who is speaking again, describing his own depression when the holidays ended and he left his brother as they went to their different schools. I expect you, too, have sometimes felt just the same.

Jack's happy weeks at home while he was ill, came to an end all too soon, and now he had to face another change. Mr. Lewis, desperately seeking another school, had at last heard of a good preparatory school at Malvern, close to 'The Coll', where Warren was now quite happily established. Warren took his public-school life cheerfully, and adapted himself to its routines. Jack was quite a different matter. He keenly felt being away from home. He knew he was clumsy and no good at games, yet he was outstandingly clever. He was what you could call an individualist, which meant that he did not easily fit into the pattern of school life with all its rigid traditions.

In January, 1911, with some trepidation, when he was thirteen, he set off on a fresh journey to England once more with Warren, to go to the preparatory school near him in Malvern. But at least he felt more grown-up now. Warren treated him like a man of the world, and a seasoned traveller. When they arrived at Liverpool and travelled south by train, Jack gazed out at quite a different countryside from that which he had seen before. Travelling near to the Welsh borders he saw the countryside was not unlike Ireland. There were rolling hills, distant mountains, and small lush meadows. When at last they arrived in Malvern and took a cab from the station to Chartres, as he called his new school in later writings—its real name was Cherbourg School—he found it was a pleasant white building up the hill above the College where Warren was a pupil. From the school he looked around him, and almost for the first time in England felt soothed by the distant views. Stretching away below were meadows and a great plain. Behind the town, sheltering and enfolding it, rose the green peaks of the Malvern hills. A sort of contentment stole into his heart, in spite of the fact that there was always the wrench of parting from Warren, on whom, in some ways, he leaned so much. But Chartres—as we will call it—turned out to be a very different place from Oldie's school.

Jack settled down into a fairly peaceful life. He found he was fed well, taught well, and among the twenty or so boarders he found friends. The Headmaster, discovered in Jack a boy with exceptional ability in Classics and English, and very soon it began to be said that Jack might do well enough to gain a scholarship to Malvern College, Warren's public school.

But here at Chartres, Jack was influenced in quite unexpected ways. One thing, he later recorded, was that he ceased to be a Christian. Strangely, this came about through the unconscious influence of a most kind and skilled school matron. The one great need that Jack had was for a mother. Miss C. the matron, gave him especial loving care and kindness because of this. She was a woman whom all the boys loved, cheery and friendly when they were well; skilled and comforting when they were ill. She never talked 'down' to them, but treated them as intelligent people, and she was quite willing to talk to them about her beliefs.

Miss C. was a seeker after truth, and longed sincerely for a firm faith. In her search she was at that time much influenced by spiritualism and anything to do with the occult. This fascinated Jack. It was almost like eating forbidden fruit. The very ideas which Miss C. spoke of, gripped him. Past misery, associated with kneeling in the curtainless dormitory at Oldie's on those blazing moonlight nights, when he tortured himself, trying to be sure that his prayers were sincere and strong enough to be answered, faded from his memory, and all the horrors with it. He now found the idea of a vast spirit world, unseen, but surrounding the real world was fascinating. Jack had always been gripped by stories of other worlds and other forms of life, but he had never believed in them. Now he began to want to know more about the world of spirits. His very limited Christian knowledge, to which he had clung, started to fade, and to lose its interest. It appeared dull beside these new excitements. Slowly but surely his fears about the welfare of his soul cooled. But his Christian beliefs cooled with them. The fact was he had never enjoyed his religion. He had let it become a burden and a torment, not a strength. He had almost driven himself to distraction while trying to discipline himself to pray so fervently that his prayers *must* surely be answered. In fact, he had driven himself too far by adopting a weary false routine which had only brought him night torments.

It was about this time also that he began to feel a pessimism, a suspicion that the universe was a hostile unfriendly place. His father's quite unnecessary and exaggerated forecasts of disaster and the need for ceaseless work and struggle, had

cast a gloom over him. One day Jack said to one of his
closest friends at Chartres that life consisted only in 'Term,
holidays, term, holidays, till we leave school, and then work,
work, work, till we die.' As if that was not depressing enough,
he still had a deep inner dismay at his own clumsiness and
lack of ability with his hands. And slowly but surely, because
he was a kind, gentle boy at heart, he became disillusioned
with his fellow-men, noting their unkindnesses to each other.
He was roused to real anger, to what he called 'the most
murderous feelings I ever entertained', when he tried to give
something to a beggar near the school gates, and a certain
master stopped him from doing so. He began to see many
flaws in other people's characters. Studying the classics he
read some words of Lucretius. They summed up exactly
what he felt:

> Had God designed the world, it would not be
> A world so frail and faulty as we see.

With all these thoughts in his mind, he gradually left all
traces of a faith behind, and found he experienced a great
relief. Poor Miss C. had, all unknowingly, helped to under-
mine the foundations, nevertheless she had given him
something he had sorely needed, kindness, affection and
understanding, particularly because he had no mother.
Then, the blow fell, she left the school, and Jack found there
was a real gap in his life; his affection had gone out to her
and he had been helped not to feel frightened of emotion.
For after his mother's death, any show of feeling had greatly
troubled him.

Various masters made a vivid impression on him. One of
whom he was particularly fond, was full of cheerful high
spirits, and turned life now into an adventure, now into a
joke and the boys loved him. It was a blow when he left at
the same time as Miss C.

Then a master the boys called Pogo came, and Pogo was
smart, humorous, a man about town; he taught the boys to

be dressy, to feel like men of the world. He fascinated them, but his temper was very uncertain. Jack began to try, he records, 'to be a fop, a cad, and a snob'.

These were the days, as he wrote years later in his own account of his early life, when he lost 'his faith, his virtue and his simplicity'. He had his first sexual experience, which he felt later was partly due to his age, partly to the fact that he had deliberately withdrawn himself from the protection of God. Then he felt his first passion, for his dancing mistress. Perhaps it was the fact that it was the last night of term, and that the intoxicating happiness of the thought of going home the next day was flowing through him. But the schoolroom was decorated for a dance. What small unpredictable events bring unexpected results! He watched her lift one of the flags, press it to her face and say, 'I love the smell of bunting.' Seeing this, he said, 'I was undone.'

Jack was growing up. He felt this more strongly on the journeys to and from Ireland with Warren, for those days became landmarks in his life. Now when they arrived off the night ferry in Liverpool, they would go to the Lime Street Hotel, sit in the lounge and smoke and read magazines or books. They would stay there—tasting freedom from their father's rules at home, and freedom from the disciplines of school—until it was time to take the last possible train south to Malvern.

Even at home he was being introduced to some new more grown-up pleasures, when his father used to take both boys to the Belfast Hippodrome. Mr. Lewis and Warren enjoyed themselves more than Jack, who did not particularly like the variety shows or vaudeville as it was then called. But he did enjoy being with his father on these nights out, for he was often in a jovial mood and he especially liked the splendid cold supper waiting for them on their return.

In later years, Jack grew to feel that the period of what he called boyhood, between childhood and adolescence, was a sort of 'Dark Ages'. It was full of noise, cruelty, greed, full of dull unromantic events. It was a time when he was not true to himself, when he did not use his vivid, fertile imagination, and when his lowest feelings and ambitions were aroused. The real person was there in childhood and adolescence, and in adult life, but it was stifled in boyhood. The 'Joy' he had experienced from time to time had completely gone.

Jack was at Chartres from 1911—1913, but before he left he broke free of this dark period, and his life opened out again, like the cold earth in spring. He later wrote a beautiful description of how this seemed to him at the time:

> It was as if the Arctic itself, all the deep layers of secular ice, should change not in a week or an hour, but instantly, into a landscape of grass and primroses and orchards in bloom, deafened with bird songs and astir with running water.

It all began when he picked up a literary magazine and gazed at a headline and a picture; and for him, as he was to say 'the sky turned round'. He read the title of a book: *Siegfried and the Twilight of the Gods*. He saw one of the delicate yet powerful illustrations of this old Norse Saga, by Arthur Rackham, taken from it. Although he knew nothing of the book, he had a deep stirring sense of 'pure Northernness'. It is interesting to remember that Ulster, where Jack grew up is a northern land, and Jack, like many from the North, had a deep feeling for vast distances, remoteness and wild lands. Now there stirred in him great visions of huge cold empty spaces above the Atlantic, and of the long cool twilight of Northern summers, where travellers may see the midnight sun. He remembered from Northern myth the words that had long before stabbed him, 'Balder is dead.' Suddenly he felt as if he was gazing into his own country, as if he was returning from a far-off desert land, and was about to take up his inheritance. And once again, as if a voice was calling him from far far away, he was filled with the piercing memory of 'Joy', of the old unfulfilled longing, of visions of unattainable beauty that he had known from time to time as a child.

The Norse legends of the Nibelungs, in which Siegfried is a great hero, were immortalised in the music of Wagner in the last century in four musical dramas. One of the best known pieces is *The Ride of the Valkyries*, those messenger maidens of Odin, the supreme god and creator. The music is sometimes thunderous, full of excitement and sombre strength. Jack discovered that the four operas were available on gramophone records. He now lived in a world of record catalogues. The northern epic had fired his imagination. Then he himself began to write a long heroic poem about the story of Siegfried, having discovered in a magazine a summary of the Siegfried stories as told in the operas. Jack's poem was a great achievement. It went into four books. But he could not finish it, because by the time he came to the fourth book he was trying, with intense feeling, to write real poetry, not just verse or rhyming lines. This experience taught him what writing really meant.

Little by little, he purchased Wagner's music on records. All his pocket money was spent on it. But he still had never seen a copy of the book whose title had so gripped him. One day he went to stay with one of his beautiful cousins, the eldest daughter of Cousin Quartus. She was married, and lived on the outskirts of Dublin. Jack describes her as 'the dark Juno, the queen of Olympus'. In her room on a table he suddenly saw the very book, with Arthur Rackham's wonderful illustrations, *Siegfried and the Twilight of the Gods*. His excitement was intense as he turned the pages. He knew that somehow, by some means, he must raise enough money to buy a copy for himself, for as he read, he was transported into another world. This ability to enter other worlds in imagination, indeed to create them himself in his writing, was to stay with him for life.

Warren, always generous, and full of a deep understanding of his unusual younger brother, eventually helped him, when it was found that a 'cheap' edition was published for fifteen

shillings. To Jack, that was wealth, and such a sum was
beyond him. But Warren shared the cost. Jack while knowing
the old Norse gods were purely mythical, had something like
a passion for them. Years later, he analysed it in this way,
and in the light of his rejection of God:

> We are taught in the Prayer Book to 'give thanks to God
> for His great glory' . . . but I came far nearer to feeling
> this about the Norse gods whom I disbelieved in than I
> had ever done about the true God while I believed. Some-
> times I can almost think that I was sent back to the false
> gods there to acquire some capacity for worship against
> the day when the true God should recall me to Himself.

He still wrote about his imaginary land of Boxen, com-
prising Animal-Land and India, now a united state which
had its own rules and Parliament, and it was filled with many
characters who bore a strong resemblance to certain real
people, including the boys and their father.

Jack's mind was ceaselessly active. At last the time came
for him to sit for the scholarship entrance examination to the
College. But he was ill in bed with a high temperature on
the day. Arrangements were made for him to attempt the
examination in bed. Against all odds, he distinguished himself, and won a classical entrance scholarship. In later years
Warren called this achievement of Jack's the finest of his
career.

CHAPTER SEVEN

Wyvern

YOU WILL REMEMBER THAT DURING THE TIME JACK WAS AT Chartres School, Warren was at 'the Coll', as the boys called it. This was really Malvern College, called Wyvern in Jack's later writing, so we will use his name for it.

Warren had been happy there. After the misery of Oldie's school, and the poor food, his letters home described the astonishing fact to Jack that at Wyvern a boy had as much to eat as he wanted. As he was more 'outgoing' than Jack, he fitted easily into the school life and routines. But at home by this time he became increasingly at loggerheads with his father. His manners were surly and off-hand with him, and he resented his father's constant wish to know about every detail of the boys' lives. His school reports grew steadily worse. His one great and continuing desire was to have a motor-bicycle. Mr. Lewis, perhaps because there was no understanding mother in the home, to interpret father to son, and son to father, and to pour oil on the troubled waters of their conflict, became angry and bitter with Warren. At last, in despair of his doing well, he took him away from Wyvern, and sent him to live with his own elderly retired headmaster, Mr. Kirkpatrick, and his wife, who had settled at Bookham in Surrey, where Warren was to be prepared for entry to Sandhurst, to become an Army Officer. Mr. Lewis was shocked to hear from Mr. Kirkpatrick that it was his opinion that Warren must have learned almost nothing at school.

Warren went to Bookham at the same time that Jack was to start at Wyvern. We can imagine him encouraging Jack in this new move, proud of him for being a scholar, and relating to him all the fun and good of life at Wyvern as he had experienced it there. Warren felt sure Jack would be as happy as he had been.

At first Jack was almost breathless with excitement and suspense at the thought of going to this great school. He was now nearly fifteen. He had sometimes been with other boys from Chartres to watch matches there, and had gazed with awe at those lofty and wonderful seniors, the 'Bloods', as the Prefects and Athletes were called. To Jack they had seemed like gods in their private world. Somehow they gave him an exciting feeling of importance and he felt almost as if he was going to worship at their shrine.

Now Jack had to travel alone. He arrived at his House, feeling excited and a little awed. It was a tall stone building. As he went inside he smelt that familiar 'school' smell of freshly polished wood, and washed stone. As he looked round at the part of the House he was to live in, it immediately reminded him a little of the Irish ferry, for here were two dark corridors at right angles, off which opened many doors just like the ship's cabins. In fact, they were studies, about six feet square, and shared by two or even three boys. To Jack, fresh from his preparatory school, where there was nowhere you could call your own, they seemed wonderful. As he peeped in, he saw they were full of the clutter dear to all schoolboys, pictures, ornaments, bookcases, typical of the Edwardian period when rooms were stuffed full of nick-knacks.

On that first day, Jack was sent to sit with about a dozen new boys in a rather dark large room. They sat huddled together, on a fixed bench which ran around a table clamped to the floor, and feeling a little apprehensive, they talked together in whispers. They knew that only a chosen few would be given real studies at first, and were anxiously waiting to see what would happen to the rest of them.

Then an odd thing happened. From time to time different boys would burst in, smile to themselves, and go out again. The only thing they had in common was that they were

rather girlishly pretty of face. Jack was to learn with some
shock and revulsion that these were known as the Tarts
of the house, who were examining the new boys to see who
might succeed them in their position as favourites to the
Seniors or Bloods. Jack learned that the Tarts sometimes
had a sentimental relationship with these Seniors, and usually
had influence with them, and were in favour with them.
Jack wrote sarcastically of this set-up in later life, comment-
ing that it did not shock so much as bore him. Warren
commented later that he felt Jack exaggerated it all in his
mind. Whatever the truth was, Jack had his first disillusion-
ment about public-school life.

His first few days were spent in anxiety, frantically trying
to find out what he had to do, and where. Most important
was to find out what 'Club' he belonged to for compulsory
games. For this he had to run to the main school, and search
for his name on a notice-board. Games were worshipped at
Wyvern, and the athletes were the school's aristocracy.
Jack, who hated games, felt a fish out of water. However he
ran anxiously to try and find his name, but the milling
crowds around the board were so great, he could not get
near enough to see it. At last, hot and worried in case he
missed the next thing he was supposed to do, he ran back to
his House, hoping to find it later. A boy called Fribble,
was standing at the door of the Prefects' Room as he passed.
Suddenly he called loudly to Jack, who stopped in his tracks:
'Oh, I say Lewis,' Fribble shouted, 'I can tell you your Club.
You're in the same one as me, B 6.' Jack was overjoyed
at what he felt was the kindness and condescension of the
great Fribble, to him, a new boy. He said it was as if 'a
reigning monarch had asked me to dine'. After this, he went
regularly to the list for B 6 Club, and was happy that his
name was never on it, and he did not have to play. Happy,
until the terrible thing happened, and he learned B 6 was
not his Club at all.

One day Jack was summoned by the Prefects for the
dreadful crime of skipping clubs. Fribble had been lying or

pulling his leg. The punishment Jack had to bear was a public flogging by the Head of 'the Coll' in the presence of the great Prefects of the school. Jack took it stoically, but I think at that moment the iron entered his soul. He saw everything in its worst light from then on. He now felt he was marked out as a sort of outcast, an undesirable type who skipped clubs, a big clumsy boy. There crept over him a dreadful loneliness, and the full realisation that Warren had gone and could no longer help him and advise him and cheer him. He was entirely on his own. Now be began to feel he could do nothing right. He was constantly told to 'take that look off your face'. Perhaps, in self-defence, he had assumed a rather arrogant bored look. It hid a deep misery and unhappiness.

Yet school work was left for him to excel at, and here he came into his own. Before his fifteenth birthday, only a few weeks after his arrival, he did so brilliant a piece of translation from Horace, that even the Headmaster took note of it. He was already placed in a high form. This was encouraging. But eventually even work became difficult for him because of the system of fagging at Wyvern. This old system, traditional in so many great English public schools, could often fill the life of a boy with anxiety and frustration. The junior boys, especially the new boys, were a sort of labour pool. When the Bloods needed any trivial or menial job done, like having their studies cleaned, or their O.T.C. (Officers' Training Corps) kit polished, or their boots cleaned, or tea made, they shouted for a fag. All these young boys had to run at the sound of the shout, and generally the least popular were chosen to do the work.

To the end of his days, Jack was never to forget the cold 'boot-hole' in a dark smelly cellar where he endlessly queued for the shoe-cleaning brushes in a fever of anxiety in case he should miss his own work, or get behind in it. Before long this sort of life left him so tired that he could not do his school work properly. There may have been physical reasons. He had been ill just before going to Wyvern. He was growing too fast, and probably outgrowing his strength. Even more, he was unhappy in spirit, and felt himself a misfit. 'I was dog-tired, cab-horse tired', he wrote later, describing those days. Now the only blessedness seemed the coming of night when he could lie down and sleep, away from the perpetual raucous sound of shouting schoolboy voices.

Even the nights were disturbed by constant toothache. As he woke, heavy and tired each morning, the coming day had the feel of nightmare.

Just about this time Warren arrived to take part as an Old Boy in a House Supper. To him it was a happy cheerful noisy occasion, and he enjoyed meeting all his friends. But one thing greatly shocked him. He saw Jack there, looking so utterly depressed and bored, not bothering to hide this and taking no part in the fun, and he knew instinctively that this would make him even more unpopular.

Jack was, in fact, turning against the whole way of life at Wyvern. He became deeply scornful at the glorified position of games in the school, and this was not only because he could never hope to excel in them. But watching the extreme nervousness of many boys as they went out to be coached, feeling their future depended on their performance, he felt they were like stage-struck girls going to an audition.

As usual, his alert mind, even when it was tired, was receiving vivid impressions, which were reproduced freshly in later life, like pictures. He had the power of almost total recall, which means that he could let himself return in memory to those days, and re-live them, seeing the characters who peopled them, almost as if they were once more in the room, or the scenes and events as if he was once more watching them, but now with the eye of the artist and some times the judge. The characters at Wyvern leap to life again in the pages of *Surprised by Joy* written years later. There was for example, the daring, high-spirited, 'untameable' young Irish earl, one of the few who seemed strongly in-different to the society of Tarts and Bloods, who always—

and presumably this was unknown to those in authority—
carried a revolver. It was his custom to play a hair-raising
game with it, a sort of Russian roulette. He would load one
cylinder, point the weapon towards a boy's head, and count
off, before he pulled the trigger. He used to smoke a pipe
in his first term, and vanish on strange expeditions to a
neighbouring city on some nights. Jack admired him because
'he passed through the Coll without paying it any attention.'

Perhaps the most important influence on Jack's life at
Wyvern, was a very fine form-master known as Smewgy to
the boys. Jack started to learn from him some of the glories
of literature, and at this time Jack found almost for the first
time there were a few other boys who shared his own feeling
of joy and fascination as they studied it. For the first time,
too, he began to feel he was not totally isolated. Up to now
his love of books had made him feel almost guilty. Surely,
he thought, he would have been more normal to have enjoyed
full-blooded novels? Now at last, he had found others who
shared what had been almost a secret, closely-guarded
pleasure. Smewgy had a great deal to do with this. Grey-
haired, bespectacled, with a large mouth that made him
look a little frog-like, he could yet charm with his voice, and
hold the attention riveted. 'Every verse he read turned into
music on his lips', Jack recorded. More than this he had a
grave courtesy to all his pupils, although he could also be
severe; but he was never unjust. He addressed his class as
'gentlemen', and because boys respond quickly to those who
are both caring and polite and treat them as equals, it was
somehow, unthinkable to misbehave in his classes. Under
Smewgy, who taught Latin and Greek, Jack began to feel
for himself a love of the poetry in the Classics, and he was
now haunted by Greek and Roman legends and mythology
as well as by his Norse gods.

All the time he was reading voraciously, and one of the
happiest memories he recorded from the difficult months at
Wyvern was that of escaping to the College library whenever
he could, 'The Gurney', as it was called. This became a

sanctuary for him, an oasis in a desert. It was hard to get
there; he might be summoned for fagging, if he was not
playing games, or there might be a match which boys were
compelled to watch. But if, by happy chance, he could slip
silently away, he found himself in the blissful silence of the
library, where for a short time he was free, because once
inside it you could not be called out to fag. All his life he
was to remember sitting at the tables there, while the hot
sun streamed in, and there was the drowsy sound of bees
buzzing at the open windows; and from blessedly far away
on the hot open smooth turf of the cricket-pitch, came the
sound of bat on ball.

Here he read not only his beloved tales from the North,
but he learned about Celtic mythology too, and, with the
Greek and Roman myths he was learning from the classics,
he now had the legends of three cultures on which to feast
his imagination. How vividly he later describes this:

There too I found ... a book on Celtic mythology, which
soon became, if not a rival, yet a humble companion, to
the Norse. That did me good; to enjoy two mythologies
(or three, now that I had begun to love the Greek), fully
aware of their differing flavours, is a balancing thing, and
makes for catholicity. I felt keenly the difference between
the stony and fiery sublimity of Asgard [Norse], the green,
leafy, amorous and elusive world of Cruachan and the
Red Branch and Tir-nan-Og [Celtic], the harder, more
defiant, sun-bright beauty of Olympus [Greek and Roman
or Classical].

In the library too, he began to study English poetry, and
was gripped by his discovery of Milton's power and strength
in *Paradise Lost* and *Paradise Regained*, and the almost
mystical Irish atmosphere in W. B. Yeats' poems. To his
joy he found one or two other boys shared his growing love
of poetry, and had indeed felt it before he had. He was alone,
in a sense, no longer. In fact, he almost began to regard

these boys and himself as belonging to a sort of intellectual élite, or superior people. Later, he said he was in danger of becoming a prig.

In spite of the outward misery of life at Wyvern, there was still too the awakening inner joy, which he had begun to experience again before he left Chartres. It was almost as if he lived two lives. There was the outwardly miserable one. Yet when he had the chance to withdraw from it into the inner life of the Spirit, he knew enchantment again. No words can describe this more poetically than he did in later life, telling how, even then, there were:

> moments when you were too happy to speak, when the gods and heroes rioted through your head, when satyrs danced and Maenads roared on the mountains . . . And the world itself—can I have been unhappy, living in Paradise? What keen, tingling sunlight there was. The mere smells were enough to make a man tipsy—cut grass, dew-dabbled mosses, sweet pea, autumn woods, wood burning, peat, salt water. The sense ached. I was sick with desire; that sickness better than health.

Jack started to write again himself. This time it was a Norse Saga called 'Loki Bound'. The characters of the gods represented true characters around him. Thor with his hammer and threats was a picture of the Bloods. Loki, who opposed Odin the Creator because he had made a world full of cruelty, was an echo of his own sadness and pessimism. For Jack, still an atheist, held that God did not exist. Yet still, in his inner heart, he was crying out to an unknown deity his anger at the creation of a world full of cruelty. This is very significant. Jack believed he disliked and condemned the world. He withdrew from making deep personal relationships because he could not find friends like himself. He was then quite happy to be neglected, if only people would leave him alone. He so much preferred a quiet even monotonous life, provided only he was free. He had grown deeply to fear unhappiness. And so there were these two strands in his character, one dark, in his hatred of school life, and of what he saw as cruelty among the boys around him; and one brilliant and happy when he was free to enjoy beauty in nature, and free to experience beauty in literature. I think more than anything else this sensitive Irish boy who could not fit in to school life longed for freedom to be himself, for freedom to be in a place where his spirit could grow. He grew desperate, and at the end of his second term at Wyvern, wrote imploring his father to take him away from the school. Perhaps it was a very poignant letter. Perhaps Jack never realised how, under all the misunderstandings, Mr. Lewis longed for his son's happiness. Perhaps also the moment was ripe. Warren's apparent failure had shocked his father: he was bitter that so well-known a school, expensive and of high reputation, had utterly failed to achieve anything for Warren, as he thought.

Jack came home for the Easter holidays to find his father ready to talk over the whole situation. It appeared that Warren had by now made really remarkable progress under Mr. Kirkpatrick. Mr. Lewis put it to Jack that in the autumn he could go to him also, in his case to be coached for an Oxford Scholarship. He warned Jack that life might be very lonely and boring, just living with an elderly couple. From his own bitter and sad experience, he tried to make Jack realise that to be alone and solitary is not necessarily at all a good thing. Jack listened gravely, appearing to consider his father's points. Inwardly his joy was indescribable. The peace and the quiet to study the subjects he loved without his tormentors around him, was a thought of blissful happiness. Jack's freedom was in sight, and because of this he went back to finish his year at Malvern in good heart.

But in the world outside freedom was surely dying. It was 1914, and a war more terrible than any before was threatening. Describing it, England's Prime Minister, Earl Grey, was to make the classic statement, 'The lights are going out all over Europe.'

Meanwhile, Warren had done so remarkably well at Mr. Kirkpatrick's that contrary to his father's fears, he was one of those at the top of the list of Sandhurst entrants, and one of the very few who received prize cadetships. Jack felt his father never really appreciated this success. The rift between Mr. Lewis and his older son had gone deep.

Soon after, Jack left Wyvern for the last time, and came home for the Summer holidays. War was declared in August, 1914. Warren, then training as an Army Officer, was recalled to Sandhurst.

The whole world as Jack knew it was changing, and for most people dark days lay ahead.

CHAPTER EIGHT

Happiness

SHORTLY AFTER MR. LEWIS HAD ARRANGED FOR JACK TO leave Wyvern, and just before he had gone back for the final summer term, a message came from a boy living near the Lewis's who was called Arthur Greeves, who was in bed convalescing from an illness. The message said he would be glad if Jack would visit him. He must have been a gently persistent boy, because years before he had tried on various occasions to make friends with the Lewis boys, but they had not responded. Now Warren was away and Jack was alone, he decided, perhaps without much enthusiasm, to visit Arthur. He had no idea it was going to be an interesting or significant visit.

When Jack went into the room, Arthur was sitting up in bed, and on a table beside him was a book which, more than almost any other, was calculated to interest Jack, for it was *Myths of the Norsemen*. Jack's eyes must have lit up when he saw it, and both boys said to each other almost at the same moment, 'Do *you* like that?' After that they could hardly talk fast enough, discovering they shared this same love for Northern myths and legend. Their excitement grew, and they questioned each other and discussed their own discoveries and thoughts. At last Jack had found a friend who could understand a taste, a love that he had begun to think was his alone. The joy of finding someone who understands you, and sympathises with you is rare and deep, especially if, like Jack, you have tended to be rather a lonely or solitary person, and if your tastes are unusual. Very often people like this are highly intelligent and sensitive. They have their own price to pay for this. But equally, their joys can be the deeper. Jack

later wrote about this meeting, 'I had been so far from thinking such a friend possible that I had never even longed for
one . . . Nothing, I suspect, is more astonishing in any man's
life than the discovery that there do exist people very, very
like himself.'

In view of Jack's beliefs, Arthur was, perhaps, a surprising
friend, and yet he was able to give Jack what he sorely needed.
For he was a kind, gentle, thoughtful boy. His parents
belonged to the Plymouth Brethren, a deeply devout group of
Christians, who live very strictly, and meet in a way not unlike the Quakers, and take the Bible literally, truly believing it
holds all they need for life. Arthur was the youngest of a
large family, yet Jack found the house strangely quiet compared with his own especially when Warren was at home. It
was, in fact, a gentle pious home, and Arthur was a talented
boy, gifted as an artist, and a pianist. He was also a great
reader.

Soon the two boys began reading together and comparing
notes. Arthur taught Jack to tackle the great novels by Scott,
Jane Austen, the Brontës and others. They went on many
walks together, and Arthur showed Jack beauty in everything, especially in little insignificant things like 'a farm-yard
in its mid-morning solitude, and perhaps a grey cat squeezing
its way under a barn door, or a bent old woman with
wrinkled, motherly face coming back with an empty bucket
from the pigstye'.

In one of the letters Jack wrote to Arthur, he recalls one
of their walks: 'I well remember the glorious walk of which
you speak, how we lay drenched with sunshine on the moss,
and were for a time perfectly happy—which is a rare enough
condition, God knows.'

Arthur was delicate, and had a weak heart and so was not
able to join the forces, although he was Warren's age. Jack
knew that before too long, he would have to face a decision
as to what he himself must do. So he made a solemn pact
with the future, against the time when he would be of an age
to join up. 'You shall have me,' he said, 'on a certain date,

not before. I will die in your wars if need be, but till then I shall live my own life. You may have my body but not my mind.'

So, in the full knowledge that the future was all uncertain, Jack entered on one of the happiest periods of his life.

The day came when once more he went aboard the Irish ferry, tasted the salt on his lips, felt the freshness of a stiffening sea breeze as the ship moved down the lough and headed out to the open sea. Now he was travelling alone and he had to take the train to London from Liverpool, then cross to Waterloo Station, and take a train from there to Great Bookham. It was, for him, a new country and a new adventure. At the stations there is no doubt he was reminded of war as men in khaki jostled in the crowds, and there were couples saying goodbye, and troops moving from place to place. But Jack had made his pact. His hour had not yet come. He was alert and looking out at this fresh place to which he was going.

His first impression was one of surprise. Surrey was quite different to how he had pictured it. The wooded scenery, the open grassy gorse-covered commons, the little valleys and hills enchanted him. The timbered houses with red-tiled roofs seemed prettier than Irish houses. They looked so cosy and welcoming that they reminded him of afternoon tea brought in on tea-trays.

When he arrived, Mr. Kirkpatrick surprised him even more. His main impression had come from his father, for he had himself been a pupil of his. Jack had got a strange picture of a soft and sentimental man, and had been very wary. It was really astonishing how Mr. Lewis had an unfortunate way of unconsciously twisting his facts in the telling, perhaps adding dramatic effect, but often giving a totally wrong impression.

Instead Jack found his tutor was very tall, shabby and thin. He looked immensely tough and muscular and had a grip like iron. He had a moustache, side whiskers, and gazed at Jack with penetration. Within a very few minutes he turned out to be ruthless in argument and discussion, exposing the slightest inaccuracy or lack of logic in Jack's first remarks. He was, Jack thought, formidable. But through those first days Jack found his measure. It grew to be like an enjoyable sparring match to talk with him. He was, in fact, something of an eccentric. 'The Great Knock', as the boys called him, had been brought up as a Scottish Presbyterian. Now he was an atheist. But one strange custom remained from his youth. He always wore a slightly more respectable suit on Sundays in which to work in his garden.

Now Jack's life was totally different from life at Wyvern. You might have found it very quiet and dull. But to Jack after his misery, this new life was bliss. He was now sixteen, and felt grown-up and independent.

He generally had breakfast at eight o'clock, and was working at his desk by nine with Mr. Kirkpatrick in the little plainly furnished upstairs study. The Great Knock, like Smewgy, was 'a chanter'. His full guttural Ulster voice—for he was an Irishman—seemed well-suited to Homer's *Iliad*. He would read a long passage, and then translate with very few explanations. Then he handed Jack a Lexicon or Greek dictionary and left him to go through the whole piece again. Strangely this method worked. Jack was soon thinking in Greek, and that was the real test.

Studying and writing went on for Jack until one o'clock, when he had lunch. The morning was broken only for coffee or tea at eleven. Mrs. Kirkpatrick seems to have been something of a shadowy figure beside her husband, but clearly Jack was well fed and cared for.

After lunch he went out to walk alone and was on the road by two o'clock. He liked this solitude, and claimed that the only exception to this was an ideal companion like Arthur, as they could enjoy the same subjects, and share similar reactions and emotions. They were so close in many likes and dislikes, and I think Jack knew that he need never fear unkindness in Arthur. So it is in letters to Arthur that he pours himself out.

On these solitary walks he grew to feel the charm of Surrey, 'the little valleys so narrow ... so many villages concealed in woods or hollows, so many fields paths, sunk lanes, dingles, copses, such an unpredictable variety of cottage, farmhouse, villa and country seat, that the whole thing could never lie clearly in my mind'.

When he returned to tea at Great Bookham each day, he had it alone whenever Mrs. Kirkpatrick was out. Those occasions he records were 'happily numerous', because at tea-time he loved to read books for pleasure rather than work. All his later life, afternoon tea at four o'clock was to assume the importance of a ritual, and was for him one of the most enjoyable times of the day. By five o'clock Jack was back at his desk, working until seven. The evening meal was, he maintained, the time for a talk or a night out with friends.

He was strangely content with this quiet solitary life. Occasionally Warren, who was now serving with the Army in France, came home on leave, and arrived in what Jack called 'all the glory of a young officer' to take Jack home to Ireland with him. They were memorable days. Warren seemed wealthy, and princely in his generosity, paying for first-class railway tickets and sleeping berths which were unknown luxuries to Jack. And when Jack was back in Surrey, at work again, it was Arthur to whom he turned for friendship writing to him once a week and waiting for Arthur's weekly letter to him which was, he says, 'the high-light of the week'.

It was to Arthur, therefore, that he recounted an apparently small unimportant event. One of Jack's greatest pleasures was receiving books by post which he ordered from London. At other times he bought books whenever he could pick one up cheaply if it happened to interest him. One cold autumn evening, when it was getting dark, and there was frost in the air, he was on Leatherhead station, waiting for the train home. He turned round idly, picked up a shabby little book off the station bookstall and bought it, just before his train came in. Once he started reading it, he found he could not put it down. It gripped him, and seemed to speak to him. He wrote about it in his weekly letter to Arthur: 'I have had a great literary experience, this week . . . The book is Geo. Macdonald's *Phantastes*, which I picked up by hazard . . . Have you read it? At any rate whatever you are reading now, you simply *must* get this at once . . .'

Jack little knew it, but this was to be a turning point in his life. *Phantastes* was a novel, romantic in form, and not unlike the myths and legends he loved. But it had something else, a hidden meaning, a 'bright shadow' which he was to call the Voice of Holiness. 'It was as though the voice which had called to me from the world's end were now speaking at my side,' he confessed later. It was almost as if, through reading it, some great change was slowly coming upon his spirit. In *Surprised by Joy* he describes it:

> That night, my imagination was, in a certain sense, baptised; the rest of me, not unnaturally, took longer. I had not the faintest notion what I let myself in for by buying *Phantastes*.

CHAPTER NINE

War

How often the sun seems especially brilliant and the day golden, just before storm clouds mass on the horizon, and the sky darkens. To Jack, in the hot summer of 1916, the great emerald waves thundering on the white strands of Donegal and crashing into the pebbly coves, never seemed more beautiful. He had learned to swim when he was a small boy; now there was the pleasure of surf-bathing in the great breakers, or watching for the waves of gigantic proportions that so often overtook him, knocking him over in the wild flying spray.

It was, in one way, a golden year for him. At the end of the winter term he travelled to Oxford to sit for a classical scholarship. He was now eighteen. He arrived at the station and set off to find lodgings, but as he walked through dull mean streets of shabby houses and shops, he could hardly believe this was the city of his dreams. At last, realising something must be wrong, he turned round and there in the distance was the breathtaking cluster of towers and spires in the distance that he had pictured so long in imagination. He had been walking in the wrong direction—out of Oxford! At last he found a hansom cab which took him to a house in Mansfield Road, after he had rather vaguely asked to be driven to some place where he could get rooms for a week.

Next morning it was snowing. He wrote to his father:

'This place has surpassed my wildest dreams; I never saw anything so beautiful, especially on these frosty nights; though in the hall of Oriel where we do our papers it is fearfully cold at about four o'clock on these afternoons. We

have most of us tried, with varying success, to write in
our gloves.'

Jack went home after the week's examinations, and told
his father he thought he had failed. Now Mr. Lewis, who
could be so difficult at times, showed him great affection, and
tried to reassure and console him. It was all the more re-
strained and understanding of him in face of Mr. Kirkpatrick's previous letters to him which had said that Jack
was 'born with the literary temperament, and we have to face
that fact with all that it implies'. Again, he had almost issued
a warning: 'Outside of a life of literary study, life has no
meaning or attraction for him . . . he is adapted for nothing
else.' It was a frightening thought to Jack. But this made the
great news which arrived on Christmas Eve all the happier.
Jack was elected a scholar of University College.

He returned to the Great Knock for one last happy term to
prepare for Responsions, a compulsory examination for all
Oxford undergraduates, which included elementary mathematics. But he failed it. He was later to say that he was
incapable of passing any examination in mathematics, as the
more care he took the more mistakes he made.

However, he took up residence in the summer term of 1917
at Oxford, as a preliminary to going into the University
Officers' Training Corps and so joining the Army. That first
term he was coached in Algebra for Responsions. It was to be
an examination he never passed.

It was a strange first term. Half the college had been turned
into a military hospital. A small number of undergraduates
lived in the other half. Two were not fit; two were too young
for the Army; one Irishman would not fight for England; and
a few others were able to be there for other reasons. Jack
enjoyed this company greatly. Some of them were to become
distinguished men. But it was an unsettled period. He did
regular military training and then before his first term was
over, he was commissioned as a Second Lieutenant in the
Somerset Light Infantry.

Jack knew well what his future might be. The appalling casualties of that First World War, the endless stream of wounded men returning home, the general air of sorrow and strain and terrible loss in innumerable homes in every town and village in England, spelled for him one thing—the strong possibility that he might not survive.

One day he had tried to talk to his father about the futility of worrying about anything so uncertain as his life after the war. It was one of those attempts he had often made to try and seek some understanding with his father. But as usual it failed, and he was misunderstood. Jack wrote: 'The conversation was a failure. His intense desire for my total confidence co-existed with an inability to listen (in any strict sense) to what I said. He could never empty, or silence, his own mind to make room for an alien thought.'

Army life, in fact, began quite well. Jack was drafted into a cadet battalion billeted in Oxford, in Keble College. He wrote of this to his father, 'When I left my own snug quarters and my own friends for a carpetless little cell at Keble with two beds (minus sheets and pillows), and got into a Tommy's uniform, I will not deny that I thought myself pretty ill-used.' The word 'Tommy' was then used to describe any soldier in the First World War.

Jack had, in the previous few weeks at Oxford, grown to love it so much, that when he was off-duty he wandered back into University College, sometimes to stay the night there, but always to enjoy its peace and beauty. He felt keenly the sadness of the interrupted life of all the promising and even brilliant young men who had left for the war, and once more he tried to tell his father how he felt, in a letter:

You can't imagine how I have grown to love Univ. especially since I left. Last Saturday evening when I was sleeping there alone, I spent a long time wandering over it, into all sorts of parts where I had never been before, where mullioned windows are dark with ivy that no one has bothered to cut since the war emptied the rooms they belong to. Some of the rooms were all dust-sheeted, others were much as their owners had left them—the pictures still on the walls, and the books dust-covered in their shelves. It was melancholy in a way, and yet very interesting.

While Jack was billeted at Keble College he shared a room with another Cadet, Paddy Moore. He found him good company, and when he had some leave, instead of going home he went to stay with Paddy and his mother. Later he got a month's leave, and again spent part of it with them, only returning to Ireland for the last two weeks. It was a step which was eventually to have far-reaching consequences upon his life. He was clearly getting farther and farther away from his father who seemed unable to understand him or his needs. Indeed he seemed—like many people in Ireland—unaware of the dreadful horror of war. Northern Ireland was fairly free of war-time restrictions. There was no rationing, and no compulsory military service, the war seemed far away.

In November of 1917, Jack sent his father a telegram which clearly implied he was on embarkation leave, and about to go overseas. He wanted to see his father for what might have been the last time, and suggested they meet in Bristol. Mr. Lewis, who had a fixed hatred of anything that disturbed his routine, wired back that he did not understand the telegram, and asked for full explanations. It was all too late. Jack sailed for France and the front without seeing him, and felt his father had not even bothered to come at this terrible moment.

Perhaps this was the point when Jack really began to turn away, in his mind, from his father and to look somewhere else for the comfort and love which his mother would have given him. It was the more sad because it happened just before his nineteenth birthday. Jack actually arrived in France, raw and new, on the day of his birthday, in the front line trenches. On the journey itself there was a ridiculous incident. Travelling by night with three other officers in an icy troop

train from Rouen, on a journey that was to last fifteen hours, with no light except the candles they carried, and no sanitation except the windows, there suddenly came a loud crash as they passed through a tunnel outside Rouen; then a loud grating sound, and the door of their carriage dropped off into the darkness. The men sat with teeth chattering in the cold, until the next stop, when the Commanding Officer came in and rebuked them for 'horseplay', accusing them of pulling the door off themselves. It was 'as if,' wrote Jack, 'nothing were more natural than that four officers (being of course provided with screwdrivers) should begin on a night journey in midwinter by removing the door of their carriage.'

In spite of Mr. Lewis's lack of understanding, Jack still wrote regularly to him, trying to make the best of life, perhaps so that he should not worry. He gives a vivid account of the trenches.

You will be anxious to hear my first impressions of trench life. This is a very quiet part of the line and the dugouts are much more comfortable than one imagines at home. They are very deep, you go down to them by a shaft of about twenty steps; they have wire bunks where a man can sleep quite snugly, and braziers for warmth and cooking. Indeed, the chief discomfort is that they tend to get *too* hot, while of course the bad air makes one rather headachy . . .

In fact, as Jack later described it, life in the trenches was 'detestable'. Often cold and soaked with rain, living in the dark except for the candlelight in the dugouts, men frequently fell ill.

On that first night, however, feeling very lost, he was taken to a vast drill hall, where about a hundred officers were preparing for sleep on plank beds. There, two kindly middle-aged Canadians, no doubt seeing how young he was, took him under their wing, and treated him like a friend. It was a help, and as the days passed, Jack met in the mud and filth of the trenches many, who, like him were scholars or poets;

some who were humorists, and some who were just ordinary kindly men. On the whole he found they were so much nicer than the Wyvern Bloods, and in spite of his youth, he experienced kindness from many. Once in the Officers' Club at Arras two very senior officers, calling him 'sunny Jim', took him off to their table for brandy and cigars. There was, amid the horrors of war, a real camaraderie and friendship, so that men stood by each other, supporting each other through the hell of trench warfare.

Many things left their mark on Jack, perhaps contributing to what he was to become. Certain people influenced him and one was a young man he met in his own battalion called Johnson. The two drew together in friendship and understanding. Johnson was a scholar of Queen's College, Oxford, and hoped to take up his scholarship after the war. Although he was little older than Jack, they both enjoyed the hours of discussion they spent together. Johnson had a sense of humour, and he was imaginative. He had a keen brain, and there in those terrible surroundings of war, he was moving towards a belief in God. In some ways Johnson's brain was as keen as old Mr. Kirkpatrick's. But coupled with this, he had the highest Christian ideals of truthfulness and even chastity, and a total devotion to duty. Chastity, of course, means purity, and is an old-fashioned word, and most often applied to those who firmly believe sexual intercourse is good and right *within* marriage. Jack was almost ashamed, and felt a hypocrite inside. Johnson, while being such a satisfying companion was so clearly sincere and good, and 'pure in heart', and all the while there was in him 'the fire of a poet' that so appealed to Jack. Jack had never thought that such high moral standards as Johnson's might be right for *him*. But now he began to wonder, remembering the faith he had left behind. Johnson, he felt, might well have been a friend for life. But, sadly, before long he was killed. He lived vividly in Jack's memory.

After a time in the trenches, Jack developed trench fever. This brought a blessed respite away from the horrors of the front line. He wrote home to tell his father: 'trench fever sounds a formidable name . . . which in plain English means merely a high temperature arising from the general irregularity of life at the front. In my case, however, after they had got my temperature down to normal I had a relapse, and was pretty ill for a day or two.'

As he lay in bed, exhausted from his illness and the horrors of trench life, Jack looked out at quiet woods and meadows. He was in hospital in a little fishing village; and when he grew better he used to look out to sea from the cliffs, thinking perhaps of the shores of Ireland, and the great Donegal beaches, wild and empty, and the gulls calling.

While in bed, by one of those chances that can influence your whole life, he picked up and read a book of G. K. Chesterton's essays. You may have read some of his poems. Now, this fearless writer of the first half of this century, was a practising and believing Christian, a devout Roman Catholic. At the same time his writing was so strong and robust, so full of vitality and often humour that Jack had to confess, 'I liked him for his goodness.' But he went on to say, 'I felt the charm of goodness as a man feels the charm of a woman he has no intention of marrying.' He later made the humorous comment, 'A young man who wishes to remain a sound Atheist cannot be too careful of his reading, for', he added, 'there are traps everywhere.'

After three weeks, Jack was passed fit to return to the trenches, in time for the final great attack by the Germans on the western front. The horror of these days was never to leave him. It was like living through the worst nightmare you can imagine. It was the tiredness and the bitter cold that were crippling. Sometimes, when moving long distances, men fell asleep as they marched. Jack did, and woke up to find he was still marching. In the trenches men walked in water above their knees. They often wore thigh gum boots, but if they should step on barbed wire, as Jack did, their boots would be pierced, and icy water would seep in relentlessly.

At nineteen, sick at heart, Jack saw men killed around him;

saw terribly wounded men 'still moving like half-crushed beetles', as he described it.

Through it all he somehow held fast, somehow controlled his fear. One day he saw a mouse trembling in terror of his feet, too scared to run away. He recognised in the mouse a picture of himself, 'a poor shivering man', in face of the enemy. He began to feel a pity, a reverence, for men in their terrible extremity.

One day, in the ding-dong of warfare, Jack found he was facing a crowd of men in field-grey who were approaching him steadily. They were Germans, and he felt his last moment had come. Suddenly he realised they all had their hands up in surrender, and he was facing a crowd of about sixty Germans who were giving themselves up as prisoners.

When the great attack came in March, shells were poured into the English line about three a minute for the whole day. Even that was only a minor attack compared with the Germans' furious onslaught against the Canadians away to the right of where Jack's battalion was positioned. Now he found that the depth of horror he had known as a child taken to see his dead mother lying in bed, returned to him as he saw corpses lying all around him.

As a young officer, Jack was cared for, wherever he went, by his wonderful sergeant. Sergeant Ayres gave him a devotion which was almost like that of a father. Jack, feeling totally inexperienced in warfare, and inadequate in face of the Sergeant's professional skill, was yet able to say that the older man 'turned this ridiculous and painful relation into something beautiful'.

In April the two men were together in the fearful onslaught by the Germans. The inevitable happened. Jack was hit, ironically by an English shell falling short, and severely wounded, and Sergeant Ayres was killed beside him.

In that moment of shock and terror, Jack found himself unable to breathe, as he thought, and believed himself to be dead.

He was carried from the trenches, to hospital. The news

eventually reached Warren, who was farther behind the lines. In great anxiety he got leave to visit Jack. By the time he at last arrived, he found Jack slowly beginning to recover. Warren recorded this, saying, 'I still recall my overwhelming relief when I found him sitting up in bed and greeting me with a cheerful 'Hullo, I didn't know you A.S.C. people got as far up the line as this.'

Jack's war was over, but the terrible memories troubled him for life. 'My memories of the last war haunted my dreams for years,' he was to write when a Second World War seemed imminent. He added, 'The flesh is weak and selfish, and I think death would be much better than to live through another war.'

CHAPTER TEN

The Aftermath

JACK GRADUALLY RECOVERED ENOUGH TO BE SENT HOME TO A
London hospital. He was still weak and felt lost and home-
sick. He had a great desire to see his father. He wrote a letter
that would have touched the heart of any normal parent.
He spoke of his desire to be sent to a Convalescent Home in
Ireland, but said it was unlikely, and continued:

> Wherever I am I know that you will come and see me.
> You know I have some difficulty in talking of the greatest
> things; it is the fault of our generation and of the English
> schools. But at least you will believe that I was never
> before so eager to cling to every bit of our old home life
> and to see you. I know I have often been far from what I
> should be in my relation to you, and have undervalued an
> affection and generosity which an experience of 'other
> people's parents' has shown me in a new light. But, please
> God, I shall do better in the future. Come and see me, I am
> homesick, that is the long and short of it.

As Warren later commented, 'One would have thought it
impossible for any father to resist an appeal of this kind'.
But Mr. Lewis was a strange man and had a deep dislike of
any break in his routine. Jack who had almost, in a sense,
stretched out the hand of a child who sorely needed his
father, was deeply and intensely hurt when his father never
made the effort to come. Meantime he had also written home
to give his father the terrible news that his friend Paddy
Moore was missing, and was almost certainly dead. This
news was to prove significant in an unexpected way.

Jack was next sent to a convalescent home near Bristol. Here again he felt his father must surely come over and see him. His letters grew dismayed: 'It is four months now since I returned from France, and my friends laughingly suggest that "my father in Ireland" is a mythical creation.'

Often he wandered alone in the grounds, something of a misfit among the noisy groups of young men who spent their time playing billiards. The endless sound of loud voices, shouting, and tuneless whistling everywhere, grated on him. Outside there was a deer park. Jack loved the quiet of these country surroundings, and sometimes he used to see through the bracken the face of a stag with branching antlers, peering at him. Then it would leap up and bound away. Now in his loneliness, he felt his father had let him down, and did not care about him. It was inexcusable. Other young men were surrounded by relatives happy to be reunited; there were doubtless many mothers full of concern for their sons, and again Jack deeply felt the lack of his.

But one encouragement did come to him at this time. He wrote post-haste again to his father perhaps hoping this time that he would be proud of him, to tell him that a collection of his poems *Spirits in Bondage*, had been accepted for publishing by the famous firm of Heinemann. He had been able to travel to London and meet the great Mr. Heinemann, he said, who turned out to be 'a fat little old man with a bald head, apparently well read, and a trifle fussy.' He gave Jack the good news that the writer and novelist, John Galsworthy,— who wrote *The Forsyte Saga*,—wanted to publish one of Jack's poems in a new magazine. It was an honour.

All this time Jack believed he would be sent back to the front when he was fit enough. But as it turned out the war dragged to its weary end before he was well enough, and the Armistice was declared, in November, 1918. There had been four years of desperate slaughter of young men, many only boys. A generation had almost been wiped out. England, although the victor, was a stricken country.

Now everyone had to try to return to some sort of normal

life. But for many, the searing memories could never be forgotten.

When Jack was fit he at last made a happy journey to Ireland, and there Warren joined him. Jack was in high spirits for the brief visit overjoyed to be free again. For the first time in their lives father and sons drank champagne together to celebrate the boys' safe return. It was a temporary happiness. Jack's hurt with his father had gone too deep. But he wrote home regularly, and did not speak of it.

Within a short time Jack was back at Oxford, a strange post-war Oxford as Jack described to his father in a letter: 'The re-awakening is a little pathetic; at our first meeting (of the Junior Common Room) we read the minutes of the last—1914.' There were many empty places.

One fortunate decision saved Jack's career at Oxford. Ex-service men were excused the formerly compulsory examination called Responsions. As Warren teasingly pointed out, that circumstance alone may have saved Jack, for he would never have passed the Mathematics. At the end of the year Jack gained a First Class in Honour Mods. reading classics and philosophy.

During that first year a situation which Warren found rather disturbing was becoming plain. On several of Jack's leaves he had gone home to Paddy Moore's mother in preference to going to see his father. After his father failed to visit him, Jack turned increasingly to Mrs. Moore as to a mother, seeking, as Warren recorded, 'the affection which was apparently denied him at home'. As soon as his first year as an undergraduate was over, instead of going into lodgings as was normal in the second year, he set up a joint home with her and her daughter Maureen. It is not clear exactly how the situation began. Perhaps Mrs. Moore had shown him the natural loving concern any mother would, before he went to the Front. When the tragic news of Paddy's death came, perhaps Mrs. Moore turned to Jack, her son's close friend, in her grief. Perhaps, and it seems likely, Jack had made some promise to Paddy to care for his mother. Whatever the cause, Jack now entered into a complicated and difficult relationship with Mrs. Moore, who became most possessive and demanding. Yet I think there is no doubt Jack had some deep affection for her. He began to call her his mother, and did not always reveal to strangers that she was not his own parent.

Warren found it all impossible to understand. He wrote bitterly of Mrs. Moore's hold over Jack, describing her as

> a women of very limited mind, and notably domineering and possessive by temperament. She cut down to a minimum his (Jack's) visits to his father, interfered constantly with his work, and imposed upon him a heavy burden of minor domestic tasks. In twenty years I never saw a book in her hands; her conversation was chiefly about herself . . . The whole business had to be concealed from my father of course, which widened the rift between him and Jack; and since an allowance calculated to suit a bachelor living in college was by no means enough for a householder, Jack found himself miserably poor.

Jack himself writes with some irritation in his Journal about the domestic chores he had to do. One day he noted: 'Got up shortly before seven cleaned the grate, lit the fire, made tea, 'did' the drawing-room, made toast, bathed, shaved, breakfasted, washed up, put the new piece of ham on to boil, and was out by half past ten . . . washed up after lunch.' Although he cannot have realised it, Jack had taken on a burden for many years to come.

In a way, Jack now led a double life. There was his life at home with Mrs. Moore and her daughter, and there was the great happiness of his life in the University, surrounded by brilliant friends, men of wit, men with a philosophical outlook on life, who could argue and talk with him, and all of them in their way influenced his future, in that, little by little, their views made him deeply thoughtful about his own beliefs.

There was a young man called A. Hamilton Jenkin, who

was to become well-known for his books on Cornwall. He taught Jack to absorb the atmosphere of any place where he might be, finding beauty or grandeur even in the grimness and squalor of, for example, an industrial town, and seeking value in all things.

One man with whom Jack argued fiercely nearly every night was Owen Barfield. Jack called him his 'anti-self', and once wrote to an American friend, 'Barfield cannot talk on any subject without illuminating it.'

A. C. Harwood was a young man who deeply impressed Jack because of his serene and happy nature. Jack called him 'a wholly impeturbable man' and had an ungrudging admiration for his courage and calm.

Jack sometimes thought over the clear fact that all his friends could be called 'good' men in the best sense. He was impressed by their unfailingly high standards, for they all believed that truthfulness, chastity, public spirit or care for the community, and good behaviour, were essential for a full and happy life. Jack admired them enough to say, 'I accepted their standards in principle and perhaps (this part I do not well remember) tried to act accordingly.'

Various experiences began to alter Jack's outlook. He had to spend two weeks with a loved friend who was going mad. Jack, who had always been sensitive, now found himself holding this man down, while he screamed of devils and hell. He was a man who had dabbled in spiritualism, yoga and the occult. Jack thought this had probably brought about his terrible condition, and was shocked, and felt it would have been much better if he had led a normal life and had not indulged in foolish speculations about spirits and the supernatural. It was a warning to Jack himself, for he had been tempted in the past in something the same way, but now, 'Safety first, thought I : the beaten track, the approved road, the centre of the road, the lights on.' His love of myths and magic and speculations about the occult were quenched.

It was during his second and third year at Oxford that Jack, as he recorded years later in *Surprised by Joy*, expe-

rienced 'more unhappiness and anxiety in my own life'. I
think there is little doubt that in some way this was bound up
with his life with the Moores. But life in the University
continued to fill him with deep satisfaction. He knew he
wanted to aim at a post in the University himself as soon as
he was qualified. Meanwhile the arrival at Oxford of new
young men often straight from school, who had no such
terrible experiences as the men who had returned from the
war, emphasised the passing of time, and Jack wrote to his
father: 'We are old, disillusioned creatures now, . . . and
only seldom come out of our holes; the young men up from
school in immaculate clothes think we have come to clean
windows when they see us.'

Jack's great success in his second year was the winning of
the Chancellor's Prize for an English essay. In his day to
day life in college he enjoyed perhaps above all the 'cut and
thrust' of argument and discussion with his friends. It
sharpened the wits and kept the mind keen. He always
enjoyed, too, long walks or bicycle rides in the country
around Oxford, and often described these with great vividness and sometimes humour in letters to his brother. In the
summer of 1921, his second year, he was writing:

We rode along the top of a long hill, where you look down
into a good, woody English valley with the Chilterns,
rather sleek and chalky . . . on the horizon. It was a grey
day, with clouds in muddled perspective all round. Just
as the first drops of rain began to fall, we found a young
man looking as if he was going to be hanged, crossing a
field. He turned out to be one Smith of Univ. [University
College] who is now gone down and is incarcerated at a
High Church Theological Seminary in the neighbouring
village of Cuddesdon. He would have liked to ask us in to
tea, but couldn't—indeed oughtn't to be talking to us—
because they were having a *quiet day*. Ye gods; a lot of
young men shut up together, all thinking about their souls.
Isn't it awful?

But as the months passed, Jack had much to surprise him in his own chosen friends, for something happened which, as he confessed, 'hideously shocked' him. Owen Barfield and A. C. Harwood came to a strong faith in the teachings of a well-known German philosopher Rudolf Steiner. Much of what Steiner wrote and taught was deeply Christian, although his work covered all aspects of life, including theories on agriculture, education and much else. Harwood told Jack that Steiner had 'made the burden roll from his back'. Far from being in any sort of bondage, the young men seemed to have found a new freedom. Jack felt as if he had been deserted. From then on there was incessant argument between Barfield and Jack, not a quarrel, but what Jack called a 'Great War', and he later confessed it was one of the turning points in his life. He wrote, 'Everything I had laboured so hard to expel from my own life seemed to have flared up and met me in my best friends.' This was because Jack felt he was being dragged back unwillingly to examine the very beliefs he had so happily rejected years before. For Jack was ruthlessly honest. It was Truth that concerned him, nothing else. Very slowly he began hesitantly to believe there might be an 'Absolute Mind' behind the Universe. This, he said, 'had much of the quality of heaven'. Day after day he argued. Day after day he felt as if something was slowly tugging him out of his old position, although then he had no idea where he was being drawn. In imaginative and unforgettable terms he describes those days, 'And so the great Angler played his Fish and I never dreamed that the hook was in my tongue.'

CHAPTER ELEVEN

Achievement

IN 1922 JACK GAINED A FIRST IN CLASSICS AND PHILOSOPHY IN his final examinations called Greats. His brilliant results however, did not provide him with a University post, although he applied for several. He saw other men successful in obtaining them. He began to despair that he would never be able to take up the work he passionately loved.

Even at this period he seemed much influenced by the needs and wishes of Mrs. Moore, and he wrote in his Journal about a possible post at Reading University for which he thought he had a good chance of being considered: 'In the evening Mrs. Moore and I discussed our plans. It was hard to decide yes or no about the Reading job, and she was so anxious not to influence me that I could not be quite sure what her wishes were—I am equally in the dark as to what my own real wishes are.' One thing remains clear in Jack's comments about Mrs. Moore, then and later. He had much patience with her, much compassion for her, and having taken on a burden, he was too kind a man to abandon it. It would seem that sometimes he was strained to the limit but he did not complain of this, as far as can be judged, even to his closest friends.

Eventually he was advised to stay on a fourth year and read English Literature as this would put him in a very strong position for future university posts. Jack was told his scholarship could be renewed for this year and was asked if he could afford to stay. He wrote to consult his father, and said, 'Now if, on all this, you feel that the scheme is rather a tall order and that my education has already taken long enough, you must frankly tell me so.' But Mr. Lewis now gave Jack the financial support he needed, and Jack recorded that his 'long-suffering father offered me a fourth year at Oxford'. Jack's gratitude was very real. It was sheer pleasure to him to spend a year studying English Literature and Language, and he wrote lively letters to his father describing his experiences. He now had to learn the Anglo-Saxon language and was fascinated to read the actual words of King Alfred which gave him a great sense of antiquity. He described a session with his tutor: 'I spend most of my hours with her trying to reproduce the various clucking, growling, and grunted noises which are apparently an essential to the prose of Alfred.'

It was in the English School at Oxford that Jack made a new friend. His name was Neville Coghill. First Jack noticed that he was clearly the most intelligent and best informed man in the class. He was witty, given to teasing but never to unkindness, and had all the old-fashioned virtues that Jack associated with chivalrous knights. In quite an unusual way Jack felt instantly drawn to him and there began a lifelong friendship. But it was another shock to Jack to find he was a convinced Christian. Many years later, Professor Coghill as he became, recalled the first memories he had of Jack Lewis. He remembered walking in the country outside Oxford with him: 'We used to foregather in our rooms or go off for country walks together in endless but excited talk about what we had been reading the week before.' He described how Jack 'would suddenly roar out a passage of poetry that he had newly discovered and memorised' and how 'his big voice boomed it out with all the pleasure of tasting a noble wine'. He recalled what life at Oxford meant for the two young men:

We were uninhibitedly happy in our work and felt supported by an endless energy.
There was no reason why we should not have been happy; we had both just emerged safely from a war which (we then believed) had ended war for ever. We had survived the trenches, the nightmare was over . . . we seemed to be

experiencing what happened to Odin and his fellow-gods when they returned after their long twilight: finding their golden chessmen where they had left them in the grass, they sat down and went on with the game.

Jack Lewis was at this time not only faced with the Christianity of Neville Coghill and other friends, but he began to find somewhat to his shock that the authors who meant most to him in his reading were also Christian. George Macdonald the nineteenth-century poet and novelist, and author of *Phantastes*, had begun it, and remained a strong influence. The poems of the great John Donne, Dean of St. Paul's in the seventeenth century, 'intoxicated' him, he said. I think Donne's own struggle of the spirit called out a response in him. Perhaps lines like these in 'A Hymn to God the Father' gripped him with their stark sincerity and honesty:

> Wilt thou forgive that sin which I did shun
>   A year or two, but wallow'd in a score?
> When Thou hast done, Thou hast not done;
>   For I have more.
>
> I have a sin of fear, that when I've spun
>   My last thread, I shall perish on the shore;
> But swear by Thyself that at my death Thy Son
>   Shall shine as He shines now and heretofore:
> And having done that, Thou hast done:
>   I fear no more.

Poetry gives what you could call the essence of thought. It speaks directly to a man's spirit. Those who have heard of or read about George Herbert, the country parson, who died in 1632 aged only thirty-nine, will understand why his poetry touched Jack almost as that of none other: 'Here was a man', he wrote, 'who seemed to me to excel all the authors I had ever read in conveying the very quality of life as we actually live it from moment to moment.' And yet, he went on to say, 'the wretched fellow' speaks through the form of 'Christian mythology'. For Jack still maintained Christianity was a myth. Herbert's poems 'The Collar', and 'Love', tell a little of what manner of man he was, so like Jack Lewis in some ways, rebellious yet ready to worship, flying from the good, yet inwardly seeking it, hating to give up his independence and hand his life over to God, yet eventually finding in God's service a 'perfect freedom'. He was a very Saint Peter of a man and intensely lovable and Jack was irrevocably drawn to him through his poetry. Besides such men, the atheist writers, like Voltaire, H. G. Wells, Bernard Shaw failed to grip Jack or to fire his imagination. And now he began to say with a medieval writer: 'Christians are wrong, but all the rest are bores.'

Neville Coghill described Jack at this time in these words,

a largish, unathletic-looking man, heavy but not tall, with a roundish, florid face that perspired easily and showed networks of tiny blood-vessels on close inspection; he had a dark flop of hair and rather heavily pouched eyes; these eyes gave life to the face, they were large and brown and unusually expressive. The main effects were of a mild, plain, powerfulness, and over all there was a sense of simple masculinity, of a virility absorbed into intellectual life. He differed in his youth from most others of his age by seeming to have no sexual problems or preoccupations, or need to talk about them if he had them.

What Neville Coghill may not have known at that time, was that Jack had had experience—he says he was at that time 'as nearly non-moral on that subject as a human creature could be'. But he had come to realise that people who thought 'that if adolescents were all provided with suitable mistresses we should soon hear no more of "immoral longings" are certainly wrong. I learned this mistake to be a mistake by the simple, if discreditable, process of repeatedly making it.' In other words, as he explained, the desire for true joy and fulfilment was not satisfied. 'You might as well offer a mutton chop to a man who is dying of thirst as sexual pleasure to the desire I am speaking of . . . Joy is not a substitute for sex; sex is very often a substitute for Joy. I sometimes wonder whether all pleasures are not substitutes for Joy.'

At the end of that year, Jack Lewis gained a First in English. He now had a Double First which was an outstanding qualification.

University College then offered him a temporary post as tutor, and in the spring of the following year, 1925, he was elected a Fellow of Magdalen College in face of stiff competition. The appointment was to be for five years. But in fact it was to last until 1954 and fill most of his working life.

The struggle to fight his way into what he had described as 'the impregnable fortress' of the University was over. But the first thing he did was to write to his father and thank him for his generosity in helping him and supporting him through the years:

First, let me thank you from the bottom of my heart for the generous support, extended over six years, which alone has enabled me to hang on till this . . . You have waited not only without complaint but full of encouragement, while chance after chance slipped away and when the goal receded farthest from sight. Thank you again and again . . . It is a fine job as our standards go; starting at £500 a year with 'provision made for rooms, a pension, and dining allowance'.

The sadness of the years had been that in some way father and son, concerned and caring for one another, could not communicate with one another. The father could not fully respond to Jack's warm-hearted affectionate character with anything but practical help, but this he had given in full measure.

CHAPTER TWELVE

The End Of The Beginning

TRADITIONS HANDED DOWN FOR CENTURIES LINGER ON STILL in the life of our older Universities. They are picturesque and full of meaning, and life would be the poorer if they were abolished. But nowadays they seem quite strange.

The new fellow at Magdalen, was admitted, as it is called, in 1925 and he wrote home to tell his father what occurred. He was ushered into a room where all the Fellows were assembled. After the Vice-President had addressed him for about five minutes in Latin, he had to kneel on a red cushion in front of him. Then the Vice-President took his hand, raised him to his feet, and said, 'I wish you joy.' Jack Lewis noted with some humour how he himself tripped over his gown on rising from the cushion. Then he had to go round the table where the Fellows were sitting, and each in turn shook his hand, also saying 'I wish you joy.'

He was now established in most splendid rooms in the college, and in a letter to his father he described how beautiful they were. From his big sitting-room he looked out onto the Grove, ancient parkland where deer wandered. A smaller sitting-room and bedroom looked across to the Cloisters and Tower of the college. He found the Dons at Magdalen were pleasant and the atmosphere less formal than at University College. He himself was completely suited to the life of a Don. Perhaps this may seem surprising, for often young people long for movement and adventure. But Jack Lewis had a happiness of mind that partly came from adventures of the spirit, partly from the pleasure of discovering what other men down the ages have said and revealed in writing. It is often easy to forget the well-known proverb, 'the pen is mightier than the sword.' Jack Lewis did not know it then but he was going to influence many thousands of people with his pen, not only in Britain but around the world.

Those first years in Oxford were times of deep private thought when he was not engaged in his academic work, and teaching and lecturing. He was always open and alert to the thinking and teaching of others, both through knowing them as friends and through reading their writings. He had come to the point when, feeling that God, if there was a God, was almost ruthlessly following him, he poetically expressed it by saying: 'My Adversary began to make His final moves.' He likened his own position to that of a chess player whose pieces all over the board were in disarray. But it was a game that took months and years to develop. The moves seemed slow and deliberate.

All this time he was a man given to the enjoyment of his friends, who loved laughter and argument. He went on regular holidays and walking tours, and at these times he was an excellent companion. Warren described him as having an outstanding gift for friendship particularly of an uproarious kind, and he described him as enjoying argument but never being quarrelsome.

A group of friends, distinguished men among them, began to meet regularly at his rooms at Magdalen, on Thursdays after evening dinner. The company who gathered there regularly became known as the Inklings, and there they read their own work to each other. This gathering became well-known. Even brilliant scholars found it quite an ordeal, although a pleasant one, to read a new manuscript there, because everyone would settle down to give it a fearlessly honest criticism and judgment, and such criticism could be ruthless.

In later years Tolkien would read his newest chapter from *The Lord of the Rings* which is now so well-known. In this gathering Jack Lewis became known for his brilliance, wit, and rapier-sharp argument.

In the first years at Magdalen life was new, and everything

charmed him by its freshness. He wrote vividly of what it was like to work in the great Bodleian library at Oxford, and around him he felt the past pressing in; he enjoyed the written request to all who came to 'Talk little and tread lightly.' Sitting in the oldest part called Duke Humphrey's library dating from the fifteenth century, he described what it was like to work in one of the little alcoves surrounded by bookcases. He noted 'a very beautiful wooden-painted ceiling above me and a little mullioned window on my left hand through which I look down on the garden of Exeter (college), where these mornings I see the sudden squalls of wind and rain driving the first blossoms off the fruit trees and snowing the lawn with them.' He always had the gift of making small scenes come to life in a few apt words.

Everything he read was significant to him. For example, because he found even the small details of life of interest, he records that the letters of the poet Cowper fascinate him, and this is because,

> he had nothing—literally nothing—to tell anyone about; private life in a sleepy country town where Evangelical distrust of 'the world' denied him even such miserable society as the place would have afforded. And yet one reads a whole volume of his letters with unfailing interest. How his tooth came loose at dinner, how he made a hutch for a tame hare, what he is doing about his cucumbers—all this he makes one follow as if the fate of empires hung on it . . .

Because he too had this talent for seeing interest and significance in the smallest things of life, his letters of this period are memorable. You could say he lived through each little event in his life with lively awareness. Nothing was unimportant. He was so full of vitality, so open to everything and everyone; and people who knew him then all speak of his tremendous gusto for his work, so that to be with him was an experience and in his writing people and scenes leap to life when he describes them.

During this time he recounts in *Surprised by Joy*, that a significant thing happened to him when he read *Hippolytus* by Euripides. The old, long-sought after feeling of 'Joy', the longing and the desire came back to him. It was this time a sense of seeing a shadow; a shadow of some ultimate beauty, and with this came the wish and purpose to press on farther towards its source. 'All of a sudden the dry desert lay behind, I was off once more into the land of longing, my heart at once broken and exalted as it had never been since the days at Bookham.' But as he pressed on in his search, he began to feel that what he had always *called* 'Joy' was only a pattern, or a track left behind by the real 'Joy'. Or it could be described as 'not the wave, but the wave's imprint on the sand'. Everything seemed to be saying, 'It is not I. I am only a reminder. Look! Look! What do I remind you of?'

Then Jack Lewis realised that he was looking for something right outside himself; for the true source of 'Joy'. Slowly he began to believe in an impersonal God, or Spirit behind the Universe. But he still did not believe that it was possible to have any personal relationship with this God.

During these years Mr. Lewis became very ill with cancer. In 1929 it was clear he was a dying man. Jack went home to Ireland to be with him. As Warren was abroad in Shanghai, the burden of his father's last illness fell heavily on him. Going back to his home (in Ireland) was always full of memories, many of them painful, and Jack wrote frankly to one of his closest friends, Owen Barfield:

'Every room is soaked with the bogeys of childhood—the awful 'rows' with my father, the awful returnings to school; and also with the old pleasures of an unusually ignoble adolescence.' And yet, as he sat in the sickroom day after day, he was filled with pity for his father, and for the strange, dull lonely life he had led after his wife died. He remembered with sadness his father's jollity and jokes which he and his brother knew so well when their father was in a happy mood. Above all, he confessed to his brother, when at last he had

to write to tell him of their father's death: 'How he filled a
room. How hard it was to realise that physically he was not
a big man . . . And now you could do anything on earth
you cared to in the study at midday on a Sunday, and it is
beastly . . .' Mr. Lewis and Jack had been very alike to look
at. In the light of that last comment, it seems possible that
the two were closer to each other in certain ways than either
ever realised.

During those last years of the 1920s his spiritual journey
had continued. One important event was when he read
Everlasting Man by G. K. Chesterton, whose writings he
much admired. But in this book he was shaken to find a view
of history from the Christian standpoint that he was forced
to admit actually made very good sense. Still he clung to
the thought that Chesterton was the most sensible man
alive *in spite of* his Christianity. But not long after he finished
the book, a man whom he called the hardest-boiled of all the
atheists he knew, came to see him in his rooms. The two
men were sitting one on each side of the fire, talking, when
this man casually said that the evidence for the historical
truth of the Gospels was surprisingly good. Moreover,
he went on to say, the recurring presence of the story of
the Dying God in the ancient folklore and traditions of
many past peoples suggest that something of the sort actually
did happen once. As this man was a thorough-going cynic,
Jack Lewis found his remarks shattering. For if he of all
people, was not totally convinced of his atheism, then *where*
could a man turn? You could say these were all straws in
the wind, hints or suggestions from varied sources which
came apparently haphazard to torment him. Yet they all
mounted up. Jack had the odd sensation that *he* was the
prey, and was being, quietly remorselessly hunted, and that
God was closing in on him.

Picture him quietly writing in his study, recalling his
dramatic yet steady retreat from all those fixed opinions he
had held so long. What was happening to him? He felt that
all his defences were going down. It made him, I imagine,

feel very vulnerable, even nervous; aware that within himself, something stupendous and of dramatic importance was taking place. And yet it was a secret silent happening. He wrote, as he usually did—with a wooden pen, with a steel pen nib, dipping it into the ink, unforgettable words that picture for us what happened:

> I was going up Headington Hill on the top of a bus ... I became aware that I was holding something at bay, or shutting something out. Or, ir you like, that I was wearing some stiff clothing, like corsets, or even a suit of armour, as if I were a lobster. I felt myself being, there and then, given a free choice. I could open the door or keep it shut; I could unbuckle the armour or keep it on ... The choice appeared to be momentous but it was also strangely unemotional. I was moved by no desires or fears. In a sense I was not moved by anything. I chose to open, to unbuckle, to loosen the rein ...

He went on to say that he felt he was perfectly free in this act of response, and then he began to feel as if he was a man of snow who after being frozen and stiff for a very long time, had started to thaw. 'The melting was starting in my back— drip-drip and presently trickle—trickle.' As he wrote, he saw much of this in mental pictures. He saw in imagination a fox running in the open tired and bedraggled, the hounds nearly on him. He was that fox: his friends and even some of his pupils were the hounds. They had all joined the other side.

Now he had to face the fact that he had always resented any idea of interference in his life. He had also feared emotion-alism. He began to feel like the dry bones in the terrible valley in the Book of Ezekiel in the Bible—there is a folk song about them—which began to shake and shudder, throw off their grave-clothes, stand up and become alive. He now, like a trembling ghost, felt the True Life relentlessly approaching the dry wilderness of his heart. His desire to be private was being stripped from him; his desire to avoid suffering, to

live out a reasonable philosophy, all were slipping steadily, dreadfully from him. He knew instinctively that the One who was the Source of Power, was asking for the surrender of his whole self: 'Total surrender, the absolute leap in the dark, were demanded.' And now, in unforgettable words, he recalled the final moment of the Divine pursuit:

> You must picture me alone in that room at Magdalen, night after night, feeling, whenever my mind lifted even for a second from my work, the steady, unrelenting approach of Him whom I so earnestly desired not to meet. That which I greatly feared had at last come upon me. In the Trinity Term of 1929 I gave in, and admitted God was God, and knelt and prayed: perhaps, that night, the most dejected and reluctant convert in England. I did not see then what is now the most shining and obvious thing; the Divine humility which will accept a convert even on such terms.

At last, after years of thought, of unbelief, of atheism, Jack Lewis came to a firm belief in God. It took a little longer for him to become a Christian. At first he started to go regularly to his parish church on Sundays, and to college chapel on weekdays. He reveals with some candour that he had as little wish to be in the church as in the Zoo! Some may well sympathise with him in this! He felt it was all a time-wasting exercise—'and then the fussy, time-wasting botheration of it all! The bells, the crowds, the umbrellas, the notices, the bustle, the perpetual arranging and organising.' He felt that belief should simply result in groups of good men praying alone or meeting in twos and threes to talk about spiritual matters. But the great question remained in his mind. Where had religion reached its true maturity? Was it in Hinduism or Christianity? But Hinduism, in various aspects of which he saw cruelty, seemed a mixture of paganism and philosophy and was not satisfactory. And what about the Christian gospels in the New Testament? Over the years he had become an expert in literary criticism, and in the study of myths. By now he was too experienced in literary criticism, he said, to regard the Gospels as myth. Nothing else in all literature was like them, and the Person they depicted was unique. Christ was this Person: and Jack Lewis slowly came to see that he appeared in the narrative accounts as if he were 'lit by a light from beyond the world'. Slowly he accepted that this was not just a picture of a god, but God. Here and here only God was made man. The myth had become fact, and the Everlasting Word had become flesh for him.

Jack was to remember with crystal clarity the day when he came to this belief. It was in 1931. Warren took him to Whipsnade Zoo, travelling in the sidecar of Warren's motor-bicycle. Warren remembered the day vividly, and felt it was as if Jack had recovered from a long spiritual illness which began in the church in Ulster, where he had only received the dry husks of religion. To Jack it was as if Joy came to him at last in all its fulness. The morning was sunny and he records that when they set out he did not believe that Jesus Christ was the Son of God. When they arrived at Whipsnade, he did. This he could not explain but said it was as if a man who had long lain in bed motionless, and asleep, suddenly awoke. It was, I think, as if life and beauty poured into him, as if he saw again with eyes that had been blind. The woods around were full of birdsong. The bluebells were in flower underfoot, and with the Wallabies hopping around him, it was, he said, 'almost Eden come again'.

The long journey, often hard and difficult, was over, Life had begun. And what of 'Joy'? 'To tell you the truth,' he wrote, 'the subject has lost nearly all interest for me since I became a Christian'. This was, of course, because it had been, all along, only a pointer, to something greater and deeper, as if it was just a *signpost* on a road, where, he wrote, 'We shall not stop and stare, or not much; not on this road, though their pillars are of silver and their lettering of gold. "We would be at Jerusalem."

CHAPTER THIRTEEN

Fulfilment—Through Work

THE OXFORD OF THE 1930s SAW A GENERATION OF STUDENTS
whose future was uncertain. Again the world was poised on a
knife-edge. The 1914–1918 war to end all wars, had utterly
failed to bring permanent peace, and now a shadow lay
across the lives of many young people, who wondered if
there was a future for them. Belief in many of the old values
and in the old Christian doctrines, was too often slipping
away. Some compensated for this by a tremendous new
awareness of need and the desire to help people less fortunate; to fight the appalling rise in unemployment; to do
social work; or to join the Peace Pledge Union; or perhaps to
work in the slums. Some flung themselves into a life of gaiety.
The night life of London and other great cities was booming.
It seemed as if for these the mood was summed up in
the words, 'Eat, drink and be merry, for tomorrow we
die.'

Among the Dons at Oxford at this time were many well-
known men, brilliant scholars and scientists. But one stood
out by virtue of his strength of character, his academic
brilliance, and the unusual fact that he was an atheist turned
Christian who actually believed passionately in the Christian
truths which so many were almost carelessly tossing away as
outdated. He was a rock of a man, big physically, but far
more, big in his whole outlook. Yet he could be ruthless in
face of sham or hypocrisy. One of his students described
C. S. Lewis vividly, and we shall call him by this name now,
for the young man Jack Lewis had become the lecturer who
changed the lives of many, and whose pen was to influence
thousands in a way he could never have foreseen:

There was a good deal of fun about tutorials. Lewis sat there on his vast Chesterfield, smoking a pipe and cigarettes alternatively, periodically beaming and bouncing with good humour in a hugely expansive way. He looked big, sitting down opposite one, with his great fist bulging round a pipe bowl, eyes wide open and eyebrows raised behind a cloud of smoke. As a lecturer he was the biggest 'draw' the English School had in the nineteen-thirties. He could fill the largest lecture-rooms . . . One remembers his shapeless hat and ill-fitting overcoat seen to peculiar disadvantage from the top of a bus . . . the big red face bulging out of the graceless clothes, and alive with a zest and intensity which won and warmed you.

He was a man who glowed, in the sense that warmth came from him. He could inspire and challenge, or cut you down if you were guilty of lazy thinking. Yet he was a deeply kind man.

It was after his experience of conversion to Christianity, that he showed a huge capacity for pouring out creative and literary writing. His output was amazing. At first he had aimed to be a poet—his first published work had been a volume of poetry, and he wrote regularly for many journals—but eventually he felt he would never achieve greatness in this field. Then he wrote his first novel, 'The Pilgrim's Regress' which like Bunyan's Pilgrim's Progress was an allegory which could almost be described as his own spiritual adventures in a pictorial form.

During the 1930s he came to the conclusion as he confessed in a letter that 'any amount of theology can now be smuggled into people's minds under cover of romance without their knowing it.' Now there came the first of his wonderful books of what we call science fiction, Out of the Silent Planet. The London newspaper The Times later described Lewis as writing 'brilliantly imagined and exciting "science fiction" long before the term was current, and using it . . . to convey

a deep conviction about God and about living...' Later
this book was followed by two more, *Perelandra* or *Voyage
to Venus* and *That Hideous Strength*. Many people were
deeply stirred and moved by these books, and one writer
described *Out of the Silent Planet* as 'the most beautiful of
all cosmic voyages and in some ways the most moving'.
Another critic found them 'terrifying and beautiful'. Over
them there shines as it were, a light from afar, 'the holy light
of Joy', as it has been described. Now at last Lewis's love
of myth, which you remember from his boyhood, comes into
its own, but is used within a Christian framework. For
Out of the Silent Planet and *Perelandra*, especially, are myths;
that is, they contain universal truth presentèd in a solemn
picture or story form to help our understanding. *Out of the
Silent Planet* describes a journey to Malacandra or Mars by
Dr. Elwin Ransom, a Cambridge don. Even his name is
significant if you remember the Words in the Bible, 'He gave
his life a ransom for many' Dr. Ransom goes from earth
(the silent planet, which is possessed with an evil spirit) to
Malacandra where all is peace and harmony, for a special
purpose. In the second book, about his journey to Perelandra
or Venus, he goes to a great task, where his very life is in
deadly peril; he has to destroy the enemy, a scientist from
earth, who is threatening the safety, peace and happiness of
Perelandra. Both Mars and Venus are described with truly
unearthly beauty. Lewis transports his readers to other
worlds, utterly remote from earth in character and appearance, yet in some way startlingly real. Through Ransom's
adventures, we glimpse the great and eternal Warfare between
good and evil.

It was startling to some who read these novels, to find
C. S. Lewis's rock-like Christian beliefs as the basis for such
powerful yet beautiful books.

All the while that he was using his gift for creative writing,
he was turning out a fantastic amount of literary work, and
it almost seemed as if the pace accelerated with each passing
year. His close and lifelong friend Owen Barfield recorded

that until the nineteen-thirties he had only two books of poetry to his credit, but after the appearance of *The Pilgrim's Regress* in 1933 he never looked back, 'but appeared to my dazzled eyes to go on for the rest of his life writing more and more successful books at shorter and shorter intervals.'

You might have thought the life of a Don in the nineteen-thirties was dull. It was certainly a life of routine and of ceaseless work. To C. S. Lewis it was fulfilment. He once described what an ordinary day was like in a letter to his brother in 1931. At 7.15 a.m. he was called with tea. After a bath and shave a brief walk followed. Then he went to Dean's prayers at 8.0 a.m. in College Chapel, which lasted a quarter of an hour. Breakfast followed in the Common Room and he left about eight twenty-five, and went back to his rooms, and answered notes or letters until 9.0 a.m. From nine until one, he gave tutorial sessions or lectures to his pupils. At one o'clock Maureen, Mrs. Moore's daughter was waiting to drive him home to the Moores' for lunch. In 1930 the family had bought and settled in a house that C. S. Lewis became deeply fond of, and it was to remain his real home for life. It was called The Kilns, because it was near some picturesque old kilns at Headington Quarry. From time to time Warren joined him there, and finally settled there with him in what was not always an easy household, although C. S. Lewis appears to have accepted it all as philosophically as he could. Warren commented rather bitterly that if his brother was 'in luck', after lunch he would be allowed to take a walk, which was his way of referring to Mrs. Moore's habit of piling domestic tasks on his brother. 'He is as good as an extra maid in the house,' Mrs. Moore would say to visitors, seemingly oblivious of the importance of C. S. Lewis's university work. After his walk, Lewis would return to The Kilns for tea, and then Maureen would drive him back to college. From five to seven he had to lecture or receive students, and then came dinner at seven fifteen. On Tuesday nights pupils came to read the great Anglo-Saxon saga of Beowulf with him from 8.30 p.m.

until eleven—a heavy day—and then he was ready to crawl wearily into bed in the quiet college bedroom. In spite of very little free time, the amount of writing he produced, literary criticism, novels, poetry, articles, and letters—from a fan mail that grew heavier and heavier over the years— was astounding.

In spite of home complications, Lewis's talent for friendship flourished. Tolkien dropped in each Monday morning to 'drink a glass'. Sometimes he received and visited friends at weekends; and there was always the stimulating company of The Inklings on Thursday nights after dinner in his rooms.

Jack Lewis's Christianity added warmth and ease to his friendships, and many of his friends were Christians also. One of his closest friends was Charles Williams, whose remarkable novel *The Place of a Lion* had so fascinated Lewis on first reading it, that he invited him to join the Inklings. It became clear that the two men lived in the same spiritual world. Charles Williams was in fact, one of the few men who had anything to teach Lewis. In his books, as in Lewis's, the theme is the struggle of good and evil, and strange and mysterious experiences and adventures occur.

C. S. Lewis's rooms where many friends gathered over the years were remarkably bare and economically furnished. Just as he had no interest in clothes, he seemed to have very little imagination in choosing furniture. In part, it was the necessity of being economical, for his share in supporting the Moores' household kept him exceedingly poor at first. This may have been the reason why to the surprise of visitors, the number of his own books was small. He seldom bought a book if he could read it in the Bodleian library. 'Long years of poverty, self-inflicted but grinding', Warren wrote, 'had made this economical habit second nature to him.' Moreover he was always impatient of the little necessities of living such as shopping, getting his hair cut, going to the bank. One letter to his brother gives a telling illustration of this, and of his carelessness about dress:

'I was going into town one day and had got as far as the

gate when I realised that I had odd shoes on, one of them clean, the other dirty. There was no time to go back. As it was impossible to clean the dirty one, I decided that the only way of making myself look less ridiculous was to *dirty* the clean one.' But to his interested annoyance, he found this was very difficult. The very humanity of the man, a sort of exuberant boyishness that showed at times, contrasted vividly with the formidable side of his nature. His friend Professor Coghill saw in him echoes of that great eighteenth-century figure, Dr. Samuel Johnson. 'Both were formidable in their learning and in the range of their conversation', he wrote, 'both had the same delight in argument, and in spite of their regard for truth, would argue for victory.'

There was also the tender side of Lewis, perhaps revealed only rarely in public. The longing for his mother had been so deep and terrible that it had left a permanent mark. It was revealed in his strange relationship with Mrs. Moore. It was also hinted at in a letter to one of the Wantage sisters, an Anglican order of nuns. Sister Penelope, herself a writer, and literary critic corresponded with him over the years, and it is clear he deeply values her insight and opinions. But in July 1939 he writes to her in these terms:

'Though I'm forty years old I'm only about twelve as a Christian, so it would be a maternal act if you found time sometimes to mention me in your prayers.' This was written at a time when the shadow of war was dreadfully pressing on people's lives in 1939. After his experiences in the First World War, Lewis regarded it with something like horror. He wrote to his former pupil Dom Bede Griffiths, who had come to belief about the same time as he had, with whom he kept up a regular friendship and correspondence:

Thank God he has not allowed my *faith* to be greatly tempted by the present horrors . . . one comes to realise what one always admitted theoretically, that there is nothing here that will do us good; the sooner we are safely out of this world the better. But "would it were evening,

Hal, and all was well". I have even (I'm afraid) caught myself wishing that I had never been born which is sinful.

The thought of possible separations, possible disasters, caused him to write lovingly to his friends. A letter to Owen Barfield shows what friendship had meant to him. 'Of course our whole joint world may be blown up before the end of the week . . . If we are separated, God bless you, and thanks for a hundred good things I owe to you, more than I can count or weigh. In some ways we've had a corking time these twenty years.'

In September, 1939, the inevitable happened. War was again declared with Germany. Life changed in many small ways. Because of the constant threat of enemy air raids, all householders had to black out their houses, covering windows with heavy dark material so that no chink of light was seen outside. Lewis wrote to Warren who was recalled to the Army, describing his trouble in blacking out The Kilns with a complicated system of 'odd rags'. Life at the Moores was further complicated by the arrival of their evacuees, children sent to supposedly safe areas from London and those cities thought to be at highest risk of bombing, and billeted in every possible home that was suitable. Now he wrote to his brother that although the evacuees were nice children, they seemed to have no spirit, as he and his brother did in childhood, for they were always asking Maureen what to do. He was often amused by children, and kindly and tolerant towards them, and perhaps, remembering his boyhood vividly, understood them better than might be expected. He wrote delightful letters to certain children, and often describes them with a sort of gentle amusement. In the Christmas vacation he went off to Somerset for a few days' walking holiday, to visit a friend. He wrote to Warren wishing he was there, and describing the numerous children at his friend's billet: 'Next morning to H's billet and collected him. His children are now so numerous that one ceases to notice them individually any more than a scuffle of piglets in a field or a waddle of ducks. A few platoons of them accompanied us for about the first mile, but returned, like tugs, when we were out of harbour . . .'

The war gathered momentum. In 1940 England, inadequately prepared and armed, was faced with what then seemed almost a certainty—the loss of a vast part of her expeditionary force in France, and the invasion of England. Lewis wrote to Barfield,

'The real difficulty is—isn't it—to adapt one's steady beliefs about tribulation to this *particular* tribulation: for the particular, when it arrives, always seems so peculiarly intolerable.' At about this time Lewis joined the Home Guard, and so joined thousands of men too old or unfit for the Army in a remarkably determined and disciplined force set up, to attack any invading army. Men gave up many nights sleep, and many evenings to training, yet still worked all day, and there was a strange almost joyful sense of purpose and unity in face of great trial and terror. People worked together in an unforgettable way. Lewis wrote to Warren about his first night on duty:

I have commenced my Home Guard duties with the 1.30. a.m. patrol on what they call Saturday morning and mortals call Friday night . . . if it hadn't been for the bother of lugging a rifle about all the time, I should have said that pleasure distinctly predominated. I had quite forgotten the weight of a rifle. We broke off at 4.30. a.m. and after a really beautiful walk back through an empty and twilit Oxford I was in bed by 5 . . .

It was in the early years of the 1940s that the name of C. S. Lewis began to be talked about all over Britain. One reason was certain Broadcast talks he gave, for the B.B.C. on the subject of Christianity. These were so unusually compelling, so logical and penetrating, that many of those who heard them were forced drastically to re-think their position, if it was one of unbelief. In these talks this brilliant man held out to the thousands who feared that life was a tragedy and a meaningless disaster in the dark war years, a sturdy reasonable hope that life had a great purpose and meaning; that in spite of man's cruelty to man, each person mattered gloriously to the God whom he so deeply needed, and so often rejected. It was the *way* C. S. Lewis put these talks over that was different from any sermon or any dull lecture. You *had* to listen. And thousands listened and their lives were altered, and they can give witness to this today. Only last year a magazine of true stories told how a woman in total despair in those years of war, the young widow of a soldier killed on the Burma front, and herself serving in the A.T.S., quite by chance picked up the book, '*Broadcast Talks*' recording all Lewis had said. She read and re-read fascinated. She then bought all of his books she could lay hands on. Gradually her life was changed, and she became a convinced Christian and as she puts it 'a miserably lost soul' was brought 'into a loving relationship with Him (Christ); from loneliness, disorder and anarchy was created a new life of peace, blessing and service in His name'.

He was also frequently asked to talk to Royal Air Force men, and they, too, were glad to hear him. The broadcast talks were given in 1941 and 1942 and 1943 in London, where there were constant heavy air raids. People had to face possible death or the loss of all they possessed each day. It was, in a way, a purging experience. That means the unimportant things in life were forgotten. One travelled light, and the things of the spirit were more important than material possessions. Perhaps this is why people listened so eagerly to C. S. Lewis. His hour had come, and they were in need of him.

Read some of his words about giving up your whole self to Christ, in his collected talks, now published under the title *Mere Christianity*. Think about them. Imagine that night after night you try to sleep in a tube station or air raid shelter because up above the shaken earth shudders as the bombs whine down and vast explosions seem to tear the very air apart. Listen to that strong resolute voice speaking to you:

> Give up yourself, and you will find your real self. Lose life and you will save it. Submit to death, death of your ambitions and favourite wishes every day and death of your whole body in the end: Submit with every fibre of your being, and you will find eternal life. Keep *nothing* back. Nothing that you have not given away will ever be really yours. Nothing in you that has not died will ever be raised from the dead. Look for yourself, and you will find in the long run only hatred, loneliness, despair, rage, ruin and decay. But look for Christ and you will find Him, and with Him everything else thrown in.

He became well-known all over England for his lectures at this time, and on one occasion gave a series of lectures to the Wantage Sisters, Anglican Nuns, at their Mother House, St. Mary's Convent. It was an unusual setting for him, and he relished it, and the inspiration of all he said was enlivened by the ready flashes of humour. On one occasion he remarked, quoting from the Bible, that whereas Zaccheus 'could not see Jesus for the press', (or crowd), so today we often cannot see Him because of the Press, a wry comment on much of the unending flood of reading matter poured out daily for our supposed benefit.

It was, however, with the publication of *The Screwtape Letters* in 1942 that Lewis reached fame. Now, as Warren later recounted, 'Jack first achieved wide public success of the kind that brings money rolling in. He was not used to this—his early penury had not trained him for relative affluence—and he celebrated by a lavish and improvident scattering of cheques to various societies and lame dogs . . . the total of his benefactions (then and later) will never be known.' It is said that he gave away at least two thirds of his income regularly.

The book was called by one critic in the *Saturday Review*, 'the most exciting piece of Christian apologetics that has turned up in a long time . . .' Everyone was talking about it. It was to become a classic in satire, and both human and divine conduct are seen in it from the viewpoint of hell. Screwtape, an elderly devil, Under Secretary to the High Command of Hell writes letters of advice and instruction to his nephew Wormwood, a junior devil, who had been given the task of looking after a young male 'patient'. Unfortunately the patient has become a Christian; and Wormwood is in trouble. Screwtape suggests many methods for reclaiming the patient's soul, and for tempting him away from God. Incidentally, Hell is well organised, and has a Training College, an Intelligence Department and a House of Correction for incompetent Tempters.

Reading between the lines, one can see the 'patient' tempted by some of those very things that had kept C. S. Lewis himself from God: Wormwood is to stir up friction between the patient and his mother; is to turn the thoughts of the patient while in prayer away from God to his own moods and feelings. The patient is to be attacked about chastity; must be made to feel that if his prayers are not answered, prayer simply does not work. Above all Wormwood is instructed to keep the patient alive, for as yet his temptations have not destroyed the patient's Christianity and there is much more work to be done on him. But the patient is killed in an air raid while acting as an Air Raid Warden. So skilfully is the book written that one can actually feel Screwtape's anguish as he describes to Wormwood the joy and bliss of the patient when his doubts vanished at the moment of death and he saw heaven, and realised it was *this* which had haunted him since infancy. There is despair as he says to Wormwood: 'What is blinding, suffocating fire to you, is now cool light to him, is clarity itself, and wears the form of a Man . . .' Screwtape even hints he is tempted to give up hell for heaven. Sheer inspiration has never shone so clearly through the form of satire nor have the weaknesses of a man's character been more subtly and compassionately portrayed. It was a book that was so full of liveliness and originality, it became a talking-point everywhere.

During these war years Lewis had also had published, in addition to all his literary work, *The Problem of Pain*, a popular book for ordinary people dealing with one of the hardest subjects in the world. How many people say they can never believe in Christianity because of the pain and evil in the world? Lewis faced the problem fearlessly and gave an honest and effective answer. He posed the argument that it was no part of God's purpose to create automatons, but he made men free; free to go wrong; free to do right. Yet it is in pain and unhappiness that a man often meets God: 'God whispers to us in our pleasures, speaks in our conscience, but shouts in our pains: it is his Megaphone to rouse a deaf world.' Here again was a book that made ordinary people think and argue. It forced them out of lazy thinking to face eternal questions.

Through all the war years Lewis's home problems continued unabated. In 1943 he is writing to Sister Penelope: 'Pray for me, sister, and for poor Mrs. Moore . . . There is never any time when *all* three women are in a good temper . . . From praying anxiously for a little of God's peace to communicate to *them*, I have been given more of it myself than I ever had before.' Warren later wrote of those years that 'for more than three decades, Jack continued to live under the autocracy of Mrs. Moore. Mrs. Moore was one of those who thrive on crisis and chaos; every day had to have some kind of domestic scene or upheaval, commonly involving the maids; the emotional burden so created had then to be placed on the uncomplaining shoulders of Jack.' Many people were puzzled by this situation. Why did so brilliant a man allow himself to be used in this way? Perhaps there may be a hint of an answer in a letter to Owen Barfield in 1947, when Mrs. Moore had become an invalid, and the burden was even heavier. Barfield had evidently written sympathetically about the situation, believing that Jack

Lewis's patient and compassionate care of Mrs. Moore was in itself a vocation. Jack Lewis replied: 'There is no problem about vocation. Quite obviously one can't leave an old semi-paralysed lady in a house alone for days or even hours: and the duty of looking after one's people rests on us all and is common form.' William Luther White, University Chaplain at Illinois Wesleyan University, in a study on C. S. Lewis suggests that Lewis may have Mrs. Moore in mind when he wrote about the need to 'willingly accept what we suffer for others and offer it to God on their behalf'. Whatever the truth may be, Lewis's charity and immense generosity was generally shown in private. He discussed his personal affairs very little.

He was always, in fact, concerned in the nicest way about any of his friends or any one in need. Many wrote to him with their troubles and problems, and he wrote detailed kind and charming letters back. Many women wrote to him, and his patient concern for them is remarkable in view of the vast amount of his University work, as well as all his private writing. What does a Don do, an American wrote and asked him, and Lewis replied:

Like a woman, his work is never done. Taking 'tutorials' occupies the best part of his day, i.e. pupils come in pairs, read essays to him, then follows criticism, discussion etc.; then he gives public lectures on his own subject; takes his share in the business of managing the College; prepares his lectures and writes books; and in his spare time stands in queues.

The last comment referred to the shortage of almost all necessities of life in the 1940s—food which was rationed, as well as clothing and household goods; and when supplies came in, there were regularly long queues of people, patiently waiting to buy whatever they needed.

In spite of a life as full as this, and he had never mentioned all his work at The Kilns, he still found time to go into great detail and to take very great pains in the letters to people who raised problems about Christianity. One letter to a lady answers ten questions at length, and with real concern. One of his answers is worth recording.

'It is Christ Himself, not the Bible, who is the true word of God. The Bible read in the right spirit and with the guidance of good teachers, will bring us to Him . . . We must not use the Bible (our fathers too often did) as a sort of Encyclopedia out of which texts (isolated from their context and not read with attention to the whole nature and purport of the books in which they occur) can be taken for use as weapons.' Or again: 'When I have learnt to love God better than my earthly dearest, I shall love my earthly dearest better than I do now.' Everything he wrote was full of meaning and sense, and made one think, and see further into a subject than before.

In another letter to a lady he wrote 'I'm very glad you've seen that Christianity is as hard as nails; i.e. hard *and* tender at the same time. It's the *blend* that does it; neither quality would be good without the other.'

The war years passed at last. Life had had the quality of nightmare for many. For the second time the country struggled to regain some normality; but people were bitterly weary, and this time very many civilians had been killed as well as men in the forces. Home life grew more and more difficult for C. S. Lewis until in April 1950, Mrs. Moore now a complete invalid and senile, was admitted to a nursing home, where she died nine months later.

Was it during the last years of the 1940s, when life at home was so distressing, or was it during the war years that the thought had come to C. S. Lewis to write a book for children, which would in a subtle way entertain and please them, as well as being exciting, but would also suggest to them great spiritual truths almost without their realising it or feeling they were being 'got at', and would inspire them with a vision of infinite beauty? Perhaps the thought had begun simply with the idea of writing a tale for his god-daughter Lucy Barfield. It was in 1950 that a new book was published by C. S. Lewis, *The Lion, the Witch and the Wardrobe*, perhaps one of the most beautiful and most significant stories for children ever written. In a dedication to Lucy, Lewis says:—

My dear Lucy,

I wrote this story for you, but when I began it I had not realised that girls grow quicker than books. As a result you are already too old for fairy tales, and by the time it is printed and bound you will be older still. But some day you will be old enough to start reading fairy tales again. You can then take it down from some upper shelf, dust it, and tell me what you think of it. I shall probably be too deaf to hear, and too old to understand, a word you say, but I shall still be

Your affectionate Godfather,

C. S. Lewis.

It was to be the first of the seven stories of the adventures of certain children who were mysteriously transported to the Kingdom of Narnia. Although it is twenty-three years ago since it was first published, *The Lion, the Witch and the Wardrobe*, now in paperback, is still selling in vast numbers. Narnia has come to stay. One Cambridge friend of C. S. Lewis, Kathleen Raine, the poet, wrote about these books: 'I have given away many sets of these to children, who accept Narnia with a passion that testifies to its truth to some world of imagination we all share. I delight in them myself, and never find they pall in however many readings children demand.'

Now all the creative imagination he had put into the animal characters in Animal Land and Boxen as a boy, came to maturity, as it were. The talking animals of Narnia are not only intensely lively and full of character and humour but some are hauntingly and strangely beautiful as he describes them.

The books had the same reception everywhere. *The Lion* was talked about, discussed and brought delight wherever thinking people met. But who was the Lion? Aslan, the great and glorious central figure in these books was a figure of awe and sometimes of fear. Read *The Magician's Nephew* and you will see he was there when Narnia came into being:

> It was a Lion. Huge, shaggy and bright it stood facing the risen sun. Its mouth was wide open in song and it was about three hundred yards away . . . And as he walked and sang the valley grew green with grass. It spread out from the Lion like a pool . . .
>
> Then there came a swift flash like fire (but it burnt nobody) either from the sky or from the Lion itself, and every drop of blood tingled in the children's bodies, and the deepest wildest voice they had ever heard was saying 'Narnia, Narnia, awake. Love. Think. Speak.'

We learn Aslan was *never* a tame lion, and to meet him was a wonderful and yet terrifying experience. One's life was never the same afterwards. In *The Voyage of the Dawn Treader*, Eustace, an unpleasant and mean boy who has been turned into a dragon, meets Aslan on a dark night, a night which changes him for ever. He later tells Edmund what happened:

> Then the lion said—but I don't know if it spoke—You will have to let me undress you. I was afraid of his claws, I can tell you, but I was pretty nearly desperate now. So I just lay flat down on my back to let him do it.
>
> The very first tear he made was so deep that I thought it had gone right into my heart. And when he began pulling the skin off, it hurt worse than anything I've ever felt . . . and there it was lying on the grass: only ever so much thicker and darker, and more knobbly looking than

the other (skins) had been ... Then he caught hold of me—I didn't like that much for I was very tender underneath now that I'd no skin on—and threw me into the water ... After a bit the lion took me out, and dressed me ... in new clothes—

And so Eustace, a new nicer Eustace is revealed, his dreadful dragon disguise torn off, and the real boy at last appears, shaken, and not so much changed as in his right mind again. Perhaps you are beginning to realise that Aslan is a symbol.

Then again, there is another clue in *The Silver Chair*, when Aslan says to Jill: 'You would not have called to me unless I had been calling to you.'

You might begin to guess, too, when you read the adventures of Shasta in *The Horse and his Boy*.

Now, the whiteness around him became a shining whiteness; his eyes began to blink. Somewhere ahead he could hear the birds singing. He knew the night was over at last. He could see the mane and ears and head of his horse quite easily now. A golden light fell on them from the left. He thought it was the sun.

He turned and saw, pacing beside him, taller than the horse, a Lion. The horse did not seem to be afraid of it, or else could not see it. It was from the Lion that the light came. No one ever saw anything more terrible or beautiful ... he knew none of the true stories about Aslan, the great lion, the son of the Emperor-over-sea, the King above all High Kings in Narnia. But after one glance at the Lion's face he slipped out of the saddle and fell at its feet.

The High King above all kings stooped towards him. Its mane, and some strange and solemn perfume that hung about the mane, was all round him. It touched his forehead with its tongue. He lifted his face and their eyes met. Then instantly the pale brightness of the mist and the fiery brightness of the Lion rolled themselves together into a swirling glory and gathered themselves up and disappeared. He was alone with the horse on a grassy hillside under a blue sky. And there were birds singing.

Yes. Aslan is a symbol, a picture of Christ, the great and glorious risen Christ to whom Jack Lewis had commited his life, his possessions and his great talents so that they might be wholly used for Him. It had not been easy to give up his old self, any more than it was easy for Eustace to be dragged out of the ugly dragon skin. But in doing so he had found life itself and meaning and purpose in all he did, so that he could say, 'There is one face above all worlds merely to see which is irrevocable joy'.

CHAPTER FOURTEEN

Fulfilment—Through Marriage

THE FINAL AND SEVENTH STORY OF NARNIA, *The Last Battle* was published in 1956. It is in some ways, the most beautiful and solemn of them all. By then the name of C. S. Lewis was almost a household word wherever English was spoken. Editions of his books were best-sellers in America, and many Americans wrote to him, travelled to see him, and some regularly sent him handsome food parcels during the time of food rationing in and after the war years.

As a University lecturer and teacher he was now famous. His lectures were so crowded that sometimes there was standing room only. To many of his students he was a figure of awe and admiration. One student said, 'he had more knowledge at his finger-tips' than anyone he had ever heard or known. An American professor, Clyde Kilby of Wheaton College, who has made a special study of C. S. Lewis, tells of a visitor to the famous Socratic Society of Oxford—where questions concerning the Christian religion were discussed and debated openly—who described him. He wore 'an old battered tweed sports coat—well worn corduroy trousers, a patterned well-washed shirt with a nondescript antique type tie. He was ruddy of complexion, radiating health, of substantial girth all over, and his eyes sparkled with mirth.' When it came to his turn to lecture, there was an immediate sense of expectancy: 'He was exciting . . . vivid images and portraits just tumbled out of him. He had no notes and spoke spontaneously with charm and lilt.'

In 1954, C. S. Lewis had been invited to become the first Professor of Mediaeval and Renaissance English at Cambridge. When he gave his first public lecture, the Master of

114

Trinity College, the great Dr. G. M. Trevelyan, revealed that it was the only time in all his experience when the electing Committee had voted unanimously for a university appointment.

Professor C. S. Lewis moved into Magdalene College, Cambridge, although he still lived at The Kilns in the vacations, and at some weekends. These were great and significant years. Even with all his new work, he still found time to write, and a new novel *Till we have Faces* appeared in 1956, as well as *The Last Battle*. Lewis himself felt *Till we have Faces* was one of his most important works, and so did certain critics. Yet, compared with much of his previous work, it has remained comparatively unknown. Among other books his own spiritual autobiography *Surprised by Joy*, telling of his early life, and how he, an atheist, became a Christian, was published in 1955. *The Four Loves* was published in 1960, in which he writes about Affection; Friendship; Eros (or being in love); and Charity (or the great selfless Christlike love described in the New Testament in 1st Corinthians, chapter 13). It is significant that it should have apparently been thought of and written, at this stage in his life; because it was in the Cambridge years that triumph and tragedy came to C. S. Lewis, and he was to have joy and sorrow through love, such as he had never had before.

It was in 1953 that an American couple, Mr. and Mrs. William Lindsay Gresham came to see Lewis. They admired his work deeply and intensely, and had corresponded with him. After a time, partly through his influence, they came to a belief in Christianity. Mrs. Gresham, known to the public as Joy Davidman, was a poetess and writer. Lewis recounts in his Preface to her book *Smoke on the Mountain* that she had once even been nursery governess to a lion cub! She was clearly an unusual and delightful person. American by birth, and Jewish by race, she and her husband had for a short time been in the Communist party, but later left it. They were people of passionately held ideals, and her husband had fought in the Spanish Civil War. Sadly, however, he became an alcoholic and neurotic. The marriage broke up when Mrs. Gresham's husband left her for another woman. She returned to England with her two young sons, intending to settle there permanently, and by 1955 she was, Warren Lewis later recorded, 'on close terms with Jack. For Jack the attraction was at first undoubtedly intellectual. Joy was the only woman whom he had met (although as his letters show, he had known with great affection many able women) who had a brain which matched his own in suppleness, in width of interest, in analytical grasp, and above all in humour and sense of fun.'

Joy Davidman as she was known, and her husband were eventually divorced, and Joy now did secretarial work for C. S. Lewis at Cambridge. His vast correspondence, the innumerable articles he wrote for many journals and newspapers, his own work and his lectures as Professor, and his notable works of literary criticism, meant that he needed the help of someone who was unusually intelligent and understanding, and here he had found it; for Joy Davidman who had had her own tragedy with the break-up of her marriage, and two boys to bring up and educate, was a deeply understanding and perceptive person. We learn something of what followed from C. S. Lewis's personal letters. As usual he never flinched from answering personally his enormous correspondence, and he never turned away from anyone in trouble. This is why he regularly wrote to a certain American lady, whom he was never to meet, but who wrote in great distress at a time of personal trouble, and whom he was able to support and help. He actually sent her regular financial help after a time, out of sympathy; and he always answered her letters in the kindest way. These letters are now published and reveal a great deal of the man himself. In 1956 she had news that clearly startled her for he wrote:

'You may as well know (but don't talk of it, for all is still uncertain) that I may soon be, in rapid succession, a bridegroom and a widower. There may in fact be a deathbed marriage. I can hardly describe to you the state of mind I live in at present . . . So you won't expect me to write long or many letters. Let us always pray for one another.'

The terrible and tragic situation that had developed with apparent suddenness, as it appeared, was that Joy Davidman had in her early forties developed cancer. By now C. S. Lewis was deeply fond of her, and saw her agony of mind for her boys' future. Clearly it all poignantly brought back the dreadful memories of losing his own mother from cancer. It seems as if, with that same loving abandon with which he had seen Mrs. Moore's need years before—although his feeling for her was utterly different—he decided to stand beside Joy and take on a new burden of two young stepsons. He wrote to the American lady: 'You can well understand how illness—the fact that she was facing pain and death and anxiety about the future of her children—would be an *extra* reason for marrying her or a reason for marrying her sooner.'

This great-hearted action was only undertaken as a kind of marriage of convenience in the extraordinary circumstances after agonising thought, and after special permission had been obtained from those in authority in the Church of England, because although there had been a divorce, Joy's first husband was still living. Clearly C. S. Lewis's first motive was his deep concern for Joy's anxiety over her young sons, and a real desire to stand by them as a step-father. Soon it became apparent that the situation was wholly illuminated by deep love between them both. 'If we had never fallen in love,' he wrote later, 'we should have none the less been always together and created a scandal.' A clergyman friend married them at Joy's bedside in the Wingfield Hospital, Oxford. She was a dying woman, and both were fully aware of it.

The details of this tragic picture are filled in by the published letters. But out of grief came, for a brief time, a wonderful triumph and joy. A clergyman friend was asked to come and lay hands on her and to pray. There came a miraculous change. Lewis wrote to Sister Penelope, C.S.M.V. of Wantage:

When I see her each weekend she is, to a layman's eyes (but not to a doctor's knowledge) in full convalescence, better every week . . . She knows her own state of course; I would allow no lies to be told to a grown-up and a Christian. As you may imagine, new beauty and new tragedy have entered my life. You would be surprised (or perhaps you would not?) to know how much of a strange sort of happiness and even gaiety there is between us . . .

By August, 1957, Joy was so much better that although she was still crippled Lewis was writing of 'a wonderful reprieve'. By November Joy was actually walking again, and the diseased spots in the bone were not spreading as before, but disappearing, and this was after she had been sent home to die in a matter of weeks in the previous April.

In the same month Lewis had written to the American lady that all was wonderfully well with Joy. Yet there was a shadow, but typically he makes little of it:

'My own bone disease (osteoporosis) will, I gather, be always with me, but I am not in a painful condition now. I'll never be able to take real walks again—field-paths and little woods and wonderful inns in remote villages, farewell . . .'

About this time C. S. Lewis took his wife to lunch with his friend since student days, Professor Neville Coghill, who later described how Lewis said to him as he looked across the grassy quadrangle at his wife: 'I never expected to have in my sixties, the happiness that passed me by in my twenties.' Lewis also told a remarkable story.

C. S. Lewis's friend Charles Williams, the writer, had once discussed with him his belief that a man had power to accept into his own body the pain of another person, through Christian love. Lewis revealed that he had been allowed to accept his wife's pain. Professor Coghill wrote: 'You mean' (I said) 'that her pain left her, and that you felt it for her in your body?'

'Yes,' he said. 'In my legs. It was crippling. But it relieved hers.'

For three years, C. S. Lewis now had a life of 'complete fulfilment', his brother wrote of this time. 'To friends who saw them together it was clear that they not only loved but were in love with each other. It was a delight to watch them . . .'

In 1959 Jack and Joy Lewis were able to have a holiday in Ireland, but by October a sad letter to his American friend told the news that the cancerous spots in her bones were returning. Just before Christmas he was writing again, 'Despite the terrible news of which I told you, we hobble along wonderfully well.'

It was spring again when his letters told of Joy's deep longing to see Greece. Both longed to stand on the Acropolis. As he wrote, it seemed mad to take her, but 'her heart is set upon it. They give the condemned man what he likes for his last breakfast, I'm told.' Somehow they got to Greece, and he wrote in April 1960, 'We did get to Greece, and it was a wonderful success. Joy performed prodigies, climbing to the top of the Acropolis and getting as far as the Lion gate of Mycenae . . . She was absolutely enraptured by what she saw. But pray for us: the sky grows very dark.'

In June, Joy became increasingly weak, but by Tuesday the 12th said she felt better. She was in good spirits that day, did the crossword, and played Scrabble. But the next morning she awoke screaming with pain, and had to have pain-killing drugs. She was taken to hospital at lunch-time, and that night, with her husband beside her, she died.

Although Joy's death had been expected, the blow, when it came, was terrible. So short, so deep, so poignant a happiness was ended. The depth of Jack Lewis's sorrow was recorded in a notebook of jottings and thoughts after his wife's death. It is a most sad and searching book, yet in the end triumphant. It is called *A Grief Observed*. To read it is almost like trespassing in a private room:

It is incredible how much happiness, even how much

gaiety, we sometimes had together after all hope was gone. How long, how tranquilly, how nourishingly, we talked together that last night! . . .'

I have no photograph of her that's any good. I cannot even see her face distinctly in my imagination . . . But her voice is still vivid. The remembered voice—that can turn me at any moment to a whimpering child . . .

Did you ever know, dear, how much you took away with you when you left? You have stripped me even of my past, even of the things we never shared. 'She is in God's hand.' That gains a new energy when I think of her as a sword. Perhaps the earthly life I shared with her was only part of the tempering. Now perhaps He grasps the hilt; weighs the new weapon; makes lightenings with it in the air. 'A right Jerusalem blade.'

Jack Lewis was not in good health by the time of his marriage. Just over a year after Joy's death it was clear he needed an operation, but he was too weak to undergo it, and he went to hospital. In October, 1961 Warren Lewis wrote to the American lady correspondent that his brother was very slowly improving, but unable to answer any letters, as he got so tired. He had had a series of blood transfusions, but was improving. In April 1962 C. S. Lewis was again writing to her himself, and told her that the surgeon had postponed all idea of an operation and he faced the life of a semi-invalid. He seemed calm, and made light of it. But his health slowly deteriorated, and the following year he became very ill and nearly died. To Sister Penelope C.S.M.V. he wrote in September, 'I was unexpectedly revived from a long coma, and perhaps the almost continuous prayers of my friends did it—but it would have been a luxuriously easy passage, and one almost regrets having the door shut in one's face . . .' He added 'Ought one to honour Lazarus rather than Stephen as the protomartyr? To be brought back and have all one's dying to do again was rather hard.' It was to be his last letter to her. Shortly after this, 'with regret but love for his College' he resigned his Chair and Fellowship at Cambridge.

At home, he began very slowly to recover but it was short-lived, and it was clear to his brother by October that death was near. Warren Lewis describing those last vivid days said that just as in their boyhood, now again they turned for comfort only to each other. Joy had left them even as their mother had. They drew close together. It was as if they were boys once again in the little room in their Irish home in the holidays, shutting out the sadness of the knowledge that a new term full of unknown prospects lay ahead. Jack Lewis was calm and brave. 'I have done all I wanted to do, and I'm ready to go,' he said one evening. The brothers reminded each other of past events and shared memories in their lives. From time to time Jack's humour would flash out once more.

On Friday, 22nd November 1963, after a quiet day, seeing his letters, doing the crossword puzzle, sleeping, he had tea. Later Warren heard a crash, and found him lying unconscious. Within a few minutes he was dead. It was exactly a week before his sixty-fourth birthday. The man whose fearless faith and vision had been a beacon light for thousands of men, women and children across the world, had gone. Less than a month before, he had written a letter to a little girl. It had these words in it:

'If you continue to love Jesus, nothing much can go wrong with you, and I hope you may always do so.'

He still speaks to us while his books remain. In a way, he has just gone ahead. The last words in the final book about Narnia might be words about himself and might indeed be his message to us:

The things that began to happen after that were so great and beautiful that I cannot write them . . . But for them it was only the beginning of the real story. All their life in the world and all their adventures in Narnia had only been the cover and title page: now at last they were beginning Chapter One of the Great Story which no one on earth has read; which goes on for ever: in which every chapter is better than the one before.

Suggested Reading

The seven books about Narnia.

> *The Magician's Nephew*
> *The Lion, The Witch and the Wardrobe*
> *Prince Caspian*
> *The Voyage of the Dawn Treader*
> *The Silver Chair*
> *The Horse and His Boy*
> *The Last Battle*

The science-fiction novels known as the Space Trilogy

> *Out of the Silent Planet*
> *Perelandra*
> *That Hideous Strength*

Other Novels

> *The Screwtape Letters*
> *Till We Have Faces*

Theology

> *Mere Christianity*
> *The Problem of Pain*
> *The Weight of Glory* to be found in *They asked for a Paper*.

Having 'discovered' C. S. Lewis, most young readers may go on with their own choice. These books are a beginning.

Bibliography

Material for this book is based on the texts of C. S. Lewis's works, in which he reveals so much of his character to those who wish to know him better. In addition I have derived great help from the following:—

Sister Penelope, C.S.M.V. of Wantage, to whom I am indebted.

Letters of C. S. Lewis, edited with a Memoir by W. H. Lewis (Geoffrey Bles).

Light on C. S. Lewis, edited by Jocelyn Gibb (Geoffrey Bles).

The Christian World of C. S. Lewis by Clyde S. Kilby (Marcham Manor Press).

A Mind Awake, an anthology of C. S. Lewis, edited by Clyde S. Kilby (Geoffrey Bles).

Undeceptions, essays on Theology and Ethics, C. S. Lewis, edited and with a Preface by Walter Hooper (Geoffrey Bles).

The Image of Man in C. S. Lewis, William Luther White (Hodder & Stoughton).

Letters to An American Lady, edited by Clyde S. Kilby (Hodder & Stoughton).

Smoke on the Mountain, Joy Davidman, (Hodder & Stoughton).

My Year in Hell, Joanna Everest, Inset to Guideposts magazine on 'Violence.'

It has been an inspiration to live with the work of C. S. Lewis over many months. His vitality leaps out from every page of his writing. I can only say that for one reader, 'He being dead yet speaketh.'

Recent Marshalls Paperbacks

MY ROUGH DIAMOND

Doris Lemon with Anne Tyler

'Not all women have husbands who turn out to be viciously tempered, drunkards, or even convicts—but some women do. It can be a nightmare to be married to such a man: the isolation of it, the shame, the loneliness you feel. And fear! Fear for yourself, for the children. How do you cope? Where do you get the stamina and endurance from?

I've written this book so as to share with you my experiences—and the lessons I learned from them—and to tell you that God is able to make all the difference.

Of course, it was marvellous when Fred became a Christian. It was the start of a whole new life for us. But maybe your husband isn't a Christian, and you're all alone and fed up. That's how it was for me for many years. Here's the lessons I learned from my marriage, and not only how I learned to live with, but also, how to help my rough diamond . . .'

Doris has been married to her husband, Fred, for twenty-seven years. Fred Lemon's story is told in *Breakout*, and he has also written *Going Straight* and *Breakthrough*.

FREED FOR LIFE

Rita Nightingale

'Today, at round 11 am I got a twenty-year prison sentence. It didn't come as a shock, but it certainly came as a surprise. I was expecting over thirty . . .'

Prison Diary, 9 December 1977

Rita's sentence in Bangkok for drug-smuggling caused world-wide headlines. But the **real** story is how she became a Christian whilst in a Thai prison and how her life was transformed.